T0146435

I DON'T HAVE
TIME

MY JOURNEY TO FINDING GOD

I. M. FREE

I DON'T HAVE TIME
MY JOURNEY TO FINDING GOD

iUniverse books may be ordered through booksellers or by contacting:

iUniverse
1663 Liberty Drive
Bloomington, IN 47403
www.iuniverse.com
1-800-Authors (1-800-288-4677)

ISBN: 978-1-5320-3510-4 (sc)
ISBN: 978-1-5320-3509-8 (e)

Library of Congress Control Number: 2017917888

Print information available on the last page.

iUniverse rev. date: 11/21/2017

To David Cole

Without David's thoughtful and encouraging words, this book might never have been released in my lifetime. It was one thing to open my soul to friends and acquaintances, but sharing my experiences with the public was not an easy decision for me.

KEYNOTE

I awoke with a message from God. During my sleep, He explained the signs of the cross. Catholics repeat the signs of the cross, "In the name of the Father, the Son, and the Holy Spirit."

God said to me, "What we think (touch the forehead), what we eat (touch the stomach), and what we do (touch one shoulder and then the other), all must be in harmony."

Before we can hear God and truly follow Him and not ourselves, all of these things must be in order.

INTRODUCTION

S ome people are born knowing there is a God. I was not one of them. As a child, I questioned the stories I had heard. I couldn't accept there was a being with that much control over our lives. The thought of someone taking it upon himself to build an ark and fill it with animals was beyond my imagination. This couldn't be true. How could people believe this?

As a nonbeliever, when I began having visions in my mind that I didn't understand, I began questioning what I was experiencing. I wondered: why was this happening to me? I realized I was experiencing something none of my friends had experienced. In my mind, I began hearing answers to my questions. I began to understand I was not alone. Something was really guiding me and knew what I was going to do before I did it.

When I tried to explain to others what was happening to me, no one could understand. I realized I was different. But I was the only one who knew it was a good kind of different. After some time, I would realize I was communicating with God. Since the beginning of time, only a select few have been able to hear God. I found out that I was one of them. I now understood why Noah built an ark. I knew he had been following that silent voice in his head.

I was in my early thirties when I became aware of something guiding me. Once I became aware of that guidance, I couldn't put it out of my life. It became my life.

I have friends who believe they have found God, yet when I say I hear God, they can't comprehend how this is possible. I do hear God. I hear Him when I am truly at peace with myself. He prepares me for the things that are going to most challenge me or change my life.

Sometimes when I awaken, I know something I didn't before I fell asleep. I feel things I wasn't even aware I knew. God has given me the gift of understanding why some things happened in the past or other events are going to occur in the future. This is how God protects me and prepares me for life.

I felt the most traumatic events in my life prior to their happening. I don't always understand the message when I receive it, but I've learned I must be patient. When He is ready, I will understand.

When I found God, one of my first messages was, "Put nothing between you and Me." Why would God instruct me to put nothing between Him and myself? Believing God gave me this message for a reason, I have never followed the Bible, even though I know it is full of good.

In the beginning, there was no Bible. They had nothing to follow except their own instincts. When I look at how our moral values have changed in my lifetime, how can I trust the Bible is truly God's actual Word? God did not write the Bible. Isn't it possible, even then, our moral values changed significantly from the time of Jesus and when the Bible was written?

I've watched persons in my life follow the Bible, trusting it was guiding them in the right direction. I can't do that. It is my belief, all too often, this is Satan's opening, and we will be misguided. Satan is extremely clever. God speaks to me without consulting the Bible. Again His words to me were, "Put nothing between you and Me."

Believing the only way to truly follow God is through listening to the guiding voice in my head, it is the only thing I completely trust and believe. Sometimes the message can come from something I see or hear or even the mouth of another. Once the message is delivered, that voice guides me and helps me make the decisions with which I can live. I don't get immediate answers to my questions, but I've learned that I must be patient. In time, I will receive an answer, even though it isn't always the one I wanted to receive. When you receive your answer, it comes with an inner peace, and you then know He has answered you. It has been a long and slow road, but it is so worth the time. My faith has only grown stronger with time.

God has given me the gift of inner peace. As long as I have that, I haven't let the devil tempt or misguide me. If I am not at peace with myself, it can only be that I have let myself become distracted and lost my way. It is then I have to communicate with the voice in my head, and He points out my indiscretion.

God guides me in what I say, do, and eat. I pay the price when I choose not to listen. No one else experiences the consequences. If I should say or do something that is wrong and am aware of my indiscretion and choose not to resolve it, my inner peace is gone. I risk my health. The body functions best when we have inner peace.

It doesn't matter how we find God, only that we do. I believe, if you really want to communicate with God, the first step must be to open your mind. You must put the Bible aside and communicate with God directly. Get in touch with yourself.

Many Christians seem to believe God favors those who follow the Bible and go to church regularly. I do neither. Organized religion turns me off. Each religion believes its beliefs are the right ones. I can't follow someone else's beliefs.

I have to be free to follow what my conscience is telling me is right for me.

God is alive and present today, as He was thousands of years ago. And today, as then, most are unable to hear Him. Busy with their everyday lives, they don't listen to the voice in their head, trying to be heard. Concentrating on other things, they have unconsciously closed their minds to God.

Trying to be good Christians, people devote their lives to seeking and praising God. They go to church, pray, and read the Bible. Many are searching outside themselves instead of listening to the silent voice inside their head. Despite their attempts to find God, they never open their mind and let Him in. And because God communicates with us through our mind, until they open their mind, they can't possibly hear Him.

I believe I can hear God because I have an open mind, a clear conscience, and a good heart, not because I am perfect. I know I am not perfect, but I am constantly trying to become a better person. Right or wrong, I try to be as honest as I can be. Tonight, God may tell me I was wrong. Tomorrow, I may see something differently, but today, you will get an honest answer.

When it comes to religion, most do not want to hear anything beyond what they have been taught or believe presently. They won't go beyond their comfort zone or even consider anything that goes against what their present religion represents. That is not having an open mind.

Having observed others for much of my life, it is my belief we are brainwashed from the time we are old enough to learn. We may not want to hear this or see it, but our religious beliefs and discriminations are two areas of major brainwashing.

If we could erase everything we have ever been taught or overheard, what would we really believe? If we had no previous teaching of religion, we would have to listen to our conscience. "Let your conscience be your guide."

The God I hear and follow loves everyone. God understands why we feel and act as we do. Being a truly loving God, He will give us as many lifetimes as we need to work out our misjudgments.

The discrimination against black people is an excellent example of discrimination passed down generation after generation. When does it stop? My God isn't sitting in judgment of someone should he or she choose to love someone of the same sex. Some of the most beautiful, generous, talented persons on this earth are gay. So what! Why does this bother many who believe they are good Christians but sit in judgment of others?

Whether Christian, Jewish, Muslim, Buddhist, and so on, all too often, we are mere extensions of our roots. Unfortunately many will never grow beyond what they have been taught or overheard as children. No wonder it takes years and years for change to occur. I find this so sad because it is my belief we are all following the same God.

When a person finds and hears God is entirely between God and that person, no one else can make it happen. God has a plan for each of us. He knows what we are going to do before we do it. He knows exactly how long it is going to take us to find our path.

CHAPTER 1

The day started as any other day. I was home, cleaning my house and enjoying the freedom of being a homemaker. Suddenly there was a loud explosion, and my house and windows shook. At the same time as the explosion, there was what I describe as a flash in my mind. The flash told me someone was going to be killed in an automobile accident. For some unknown reason, I looked at the clock. It was two forty-two in the afternoon.

When I later asked my neighbors if they had heard the explosion, no one knew what I was talking about. Not one person heard an explosion. No other houses shook. When I explained to friends what had happened, including the vision, several tried to convince me I had imagined the entire thing. But I knew I hadn't imagined it. When it happened, my body felt sad, as though I had lost someone. The entire thing was very real to me and upset me terribly.

About one month later, while a friend was visiting at my house, again there was an explosion. My house shook, and again I had a flash in my mind. Again the flash told me someone was going to be killed in an accident. It was two forty-two in the afternoon.

My friend also heard the explosion and said, "Yes, the house did shake."

It was proof I had not imagined this. Again my body felt sad, as though I had already lost someone.

For months, this was something I would often talk about with friends. It really upset me, and no one could explain why this happened or what it meant. I wanted someone to say, "Yes, something like that happened to me."

But no one had ever experienced anything like what I was talking about. Not one person knew anyone to whom something like this had happened.

Later that same year, I awoke in the morning with the feeling someone close to me had passed away. For days, my body would feel deep sorrow, as though someone had already died and I was in mourning. Then after three or four days, the mood would lift, and I would feel as though I were pregnant.

Again I spoke to anyone who would listen about what was occurring in my body. No one could explain what was happening. I so wanted to find someone who had experienced something similar and could explain what was happening. I knew I wasn't imagining these things. They were very real.

With the new awareness happening in my body, I began to listen to what my body was telling me. I was playing tennis three or four days a week. I had never been conscious about my diet. I was always an active person. I had two kids and helped my husband build three homes. But time was catching up with me. I found I could no longer work nonstop. After tennis, I was totally exhausted, unable to do anything except rest. I used to clean my house in a day. Now I could only work for a very short period of time, and I had to sit down. Since I was unable to bounce back, my doctor scheduled a test for hypoglycemia. It was a five-hour test.

As I sat in the doctor's office, awaiting the results, a lady was playing with a deck of cards. She asked if she could read my fortune with the cards. Never one to believe this sort of thing, I said "Okay."

As she read the cards, I could not believe what I was hearing. She stated, "Someone you know is going to be killed in an automobile accident. She went on, "You are going to lose someone close to you. This is going to upset you very much. The person has dark brown hair. "Her words really surprised me. She had just repeated my visions to me. There was no way she could have known about my previous revelations.

Even before my visions, I had feared for my father and his driving. My father was an alcoholic. I had always feared he would kill, either himself or someone else, while driving drunk. Not understanding what God was trying to tell me, I believed the two visions must be one event. But I couldn't be sure. I would ask my conscience over and over again, "What are you trying to tell me?"

Those visions would take over my life. I was constantly trying to figure out what was happening. I couldn't let go of it. I knew I was going to lose someone whom I cared about, and that troubled me greatly.

After much thought and the passage of time, I realized my father no longer had brown hair. His hair was now gray. It was not my father.

While dating my husband, I had joined the Catholic Church. Even though I attended church every week for nearly fifteen years, I never felt a connection to the church. It was something I did to appease my husband. I was not sure I believed in God. In fact, I would have said, "No, I don't believe in God."

Now years later, I knew something was guiding me, something of which I had never been aware. I now know there is a God and He is aware of my deepest fears, one of which is the death of someone close to me. I knew I was being prepared for something that would change my life forever. Wanting to understand what God was trying to divulge to me, it was my belief He was telling me this person's soul was going to be reborn to me, which was why I always felt pregnant after experiencing the death.

I am certain everyone thought I was having a nervous breakdown, but I knew what I was feeling was real. I was certain someone I cared about was going to leave me. I knew because my body had already begun mourning. And because the person was close to me and had dark brown hair, if it weren't my father, I began to believe it was my tennis buddy. I was probably with her four days a week, playing tennis.

My friend was a happy person. She made me laugh like no one I had ever known. She was a very good person. Both of us were very competitive when it came to tennis. I had some of the best times of my life with her. Although she was more than ten years younger than I was, we seemed to have a lot in common. Both of us loved our tennis. It would have upset me terribly to lose her.

Before I became hypoglycemic, I had never paid attention to my body. Fortunately, even though I had terrible eating habits, I had always been healthy. For years, I had lived on junk food and pop. Now since I had depleted my body of many necessary nutrients, my body broke down. I now had to listen to my body.

As I learned to listen to my conscience, I was guided to reading materials that would help me understand my body and what I was lacking. My eating habits changed dramatically. I avoided sugar as much as possible. I had always eaten too much sugar. It seemed, the less sugar I ate, the more relaxed my body became. And the more relaxed I became, the more psychic I became. Months later, I unexpectedly became pregnant, and my visions would again dominate my thoughts.

Believing the person I was going to lose would be reborn to me, I was certain I would lose my friend before the baby was born. I know it sounds crazy, even to me. But that was what was on my mind. As I went into labor months later, I was especially stressed.

Whatever God was trying to tell me, it wasn't that I was going to lose my friend. I gave birth, and thank God, my friend was still here. I was driving myself crazy trying to figure out what my visions were all about. I was certain there was a reason I had gone through this. For the life of me, I just couldn't figure it out.

CHAPTER 2

I t has been more than forty years since I experienced my visions. God has since explained each, and having experienced them so long beforehand made it so much easier to accept when they actually happened. For me, the visions were the beginning of my life. I assume this is what they mean when they talk about someone being reborn. It took God shaking my house and planting a vision in my mind before I opened my mind and was able to see the light.

One doesn't become a good person just because he or she has found God. It takes many years of conscience examination of previous bad decisions. Eventually you decide you can do better, and you gradually change the person inside of you. At least that is the way it was for me.

When I look back over my life, certain moments will always remain in my mind. I have to go back to the beginning to really appreciate how far I have come in this lifetime. Recalling my childhood, before elementary school, was a happy time. We lived in a very small, isolated neighborhood of about six homes. Except for one family, we were all related.

My grandfather's farm was the first home, and the family built additional homes around the farm. Some were from my mother's side of the family; others were from my father's side of the family. I would spend my childhood playing with my cousins and the three unrelated neighbor boys. Those were the good old days, spent playing games outside in the fresh air or building huts in the straw or hay in my grandfather's barn. Life was good.

Feeling secure in our small neighborhood, when I began my first year of school, I didn't want to leave home. Because I can remember things that happened in the first grade, I am aware of how even the smallest event can remain with us forever. For me, one of those events would probably be meaningless to most but is probably the most special moment I can remember between my older sister and myself.

My first grade teacher had a rule, "Drink your milk or no recess." Having swallowed sour white milk too often at home, I could drink chocolate milk, but not white. Sometimes I had no choice but to take the white milk. For me, this meant no recess.

Knowing my predicament, my older sister Pat would stop by my classroom on her way to recess and drink my milk so I might go outside with the other kids. Sadly, because my sister and I would grow up constantly bickering with one another, this is one of the most loving memories I have of her. This would be before both of us decided we didn't like one another. As we grew older, we would never become close.

Today when I think of Pat, I wonder where she was while the rest of us were outside playing. She was never with us. I have no idea where she was. Now, many years later, I wonder what she was doing.

In the second grade, my closest friend was moving away at the end of the school year. I was devastated. Much more aware of the direct connection between my emotions and my health, I truly believe this was a contributing factor in my becoming ill with scarlet fever.

My next memorable event would be in the fifth grade. I had been held over for a music lesson in another part of the school and was late getting back to class. Obviously the teacher believed I was late because I chose to be late, and having already given the class the instructions for the test, she was not about to repeat anything. Because I underlined the answers instead of circling them, I flunked the exam.

Always a good student, as a fifth grader, I found the entire situation very upsetting. I had done nothing wrong, but the teacher obviously did not believe me and was not about to change my grade. The lessons I learned from this teacher were not positive. I learned at a very young age that sometimes you just can't win. To this day, I know there are some who just shouldn't be teaching. Even as small children, we begin to make observations about life and to shape the person we are to become.

When I entered junior high school, my life would begin to change. My personality began to transform. I would lose touch with most of the girls with whom I had been friends all through elementary school. I instead chose a select few, who have remained in my circle to this day. If I had it to do over again, I would not have ignored the many friends I had before becoming part of a clique.

The good, happy days would become a memory. My grades would begin to dip somewhat. It became harder to concentrate on schoolwork. School was no longer my priority. My home life would dominate my thoughts.

Life at home would never again be as I'd once remembered it. If there had been problems previously, I hadn't noticed. But now things were so out of control that I couldn't ignore it. These days, it seemed my father was always in a bad mood. He was seldom home for dinner, and when he was, it was unpleasant. Tension filled every day at our house.

Dad had quit his regular job and was now a self-employed plumber. This left him to do what he wanted when he wanted.

And what he wanted to do most these days was drink. Between his drinking and his hobby, which was boating, it seemed there was never enough money to make ends meet at our house. As a result, my mother worked most of the time. She made sure the utility bills got paid. Seldom was any money left for unnecessary things.

Dad usually did not come home until after the local tavern closed. When he came through the door, it was routine for my parents to have yet another fight over his drinking and money. At least four nights a week, this would be our life.

It would be two in the morning, and the screaming would go on and on. My sisters and I were upstairs and could hear everything. I couldn't imagine what it was like for my brother, Bud. He was in the room downstairs, next to Mom and Dad. My brother is four years younger than I am, and I was having a hard time dealing with our environment. What was this doing to him?

After only a short night's sleep, my mother would get up and go to work. My sisters, brother, and I would get up and go to school. My father would be sound asleep. He would wake when he felt like it. Tonight or the next, we would do it all over again.

With our sleep interrupted more often than not, it was taking a toll on all of us. Only someone who has grown up in an alcoholic household can truly understand. Until you have lived with this day after day, month after month, and year after year, you do not know what it does to you. It leaves scars that, for some, will never be healed. To this day, I will not drink, and I am very uncomfortable around someone when I know he or she is under the influence of alcohol.

About the only time there was money for extras at our house was when my grandfather would give my mother some. This would happen on several occasions, and he would give

Mom a substantial amount. This was when we would get a new car or replace the worn-out furniture.

As very young children, we never took a family vacation. Mom and Dad would occasionally get away for a few days alone, but Dad never wanted to take his kids along. He preferred to leave us home or with one of their friends.

As we got older, because the most important thing in my father's life was his boat, we would go boating as often as he could get away. For me, the rides to and from the lake were always stressful. My eyes were always glued to the road in front of us. My father thought he had to pass everyone on the road. He had no patience. With four kids in the car and pulling a boat, he had to be the lead vehicle. He couldn't follow anyone.

As we got older, instead of the local lakes, we would often go to Lake Erie. I never thought of our trips to Lake Erie as a vacation. Pitching a tent, sleeping on the ground, cooking on a camp stove, and showering in a public shower were not my idea of a vacation. This was dirty and more work than staying home.

Although my dad had a boat for most of my childhood, I was never once given the opportunity to try skiing behind that boat. As a family, we seldom went for a boat ride. Dad didn't think about his kids. It was all about him. He needed to get away and relax. We would be left to swim at the state park.

Although we had gone to the lake for the weekend, next week Mom and Dad would fight because there wasn't any money to pay for the groceries, the utilities, or his plumbing supply bills.

As I entered junior high, for a few short years, my father surprisingly abandoned his trips to the lake and his boating. He had decided to build a custard stand across the street from the local beach. During the spring and summer hours, my mother would work daily from eleven in the morning until close. My sister and I would rotate. We either worked from ten or eleven till five in the afternoon or five in the afternoon till close. During the summer vacation, we worked seven days a week. While we worked, my father would be across the street, at the local tavern. He was seldom involved with the custard stand. For the summer's work, I received two bathing suits and a pass to the beach. We didn't receive an allowance or a wage.

I enjoyed my time at the beach. That was where my friends were, and I wanted to be with them. When not doing the laundry, cleaning the house, or working at the custard stand, I would be at the beach. In my spare time, I babysat for spending money.

By the time I began my freshman year in high school, I could no longer hide my dislike for my father. It was written all over my face every time I looked at him. I had zero respect for him. He would so often stumble into the house, unable to walk straight or talk without garbling his words. He would find something he wasn't happy about in the house and start an argument with my mother, my brother, or myself. He left my sisters alone. They were smart enough to keep their mouths shut. My mother, brother, and I couldn't. We'd give him the argument he wanted. I was often getting slapped because of a look on my face. I couldn't help it. My feelings and disrespect were written there for him to see, as clear as day.

I hated the way he treated my mother. He called her names I felt she didn't deserve. How could she crawl into bed with him night after night? Why did she let him degrade her in front of others by putting his hands in her clothes or in places that belonged in the bedroom between only the two of them? Why did my mother stay?

I was disgusted as I watched my father answer the phone in the dining room, stark naked. We girls were in high school. What was wrong with this man? I would never understand why he was so nasty to all of us. God, I hated him.

I believe we were in the second year of running the custard stand when we were having a particularly hot spell. For days, the temperature was in the nineties. I asked my sister if she would take my swimsuit to the custard stand with her so I wouldn't have to carry it when I walked to work. The custard stand was about one mile from our house. It wasn't a big deal. She could leave it in the car.

My father overheard me ask her to take the swimsuit. He started yelling at me, "The custard stand is not a beach house. You can carry the damn thing down when you come down."

What was the big deal? Again, I couldn't believe my ears. He was screaming over my bathing suit being at the custard stand. That was just how crazy our life had become.

Feeling totally disgusted with my father, I headed for the basement. It was my turn to do the laundry. As I went down the stairs, I ever so softly mumbled one word, "queer." Unknown to me, my father had moved to the top of the stairs and overheard me.

He flew down those stairs and began beating me in a way he had never hit me before. He was like a crazy man. He had his arm around my body until my mouth was at his back. He was really hurting me, and I had to defend myself as best as I could. Unable to do anything else, I bit him in his back as hard as I could.

For the first and only time in her life, my mother got between my father and me. I am certain she was afraid for me, or she would not have gotten involved. When I said "queer," I meant it as odd or stupid. I certainly wasn't calling my father a queer.

When my father died many years later, he still had my teeth prints in his back. I would never feel guilty for biting him. I felt I hadn't done anything to deserve the beating I got that day. The whole thing was crazy.

When the custard stand was closed for the season, we were back to our usual routine. Mom was working another job, we were in school, and Dad was drinking.

One of my classmates asked me out. I was dressed and waiting for him to pick me up. When my father came home, we got into our usual argument over nothing. He screamed at me, "You are not going anywhere. Get to your room."

I stated, "I am going out. I need to call my date and tell him I can't go."

Dad wouldn't hear of it. "Get to your room!" Being his usual unreasonable self, as the only phone was in the dining room downstairs, I was unable to call my date.

I went to my room as ordered. I couldn't let my date come to the house to pick me up. Who knew what sort of scene Dad would create? I had to call my date. Not knowing what else to do, I climbed out my bedroom window and down the television antenna tower. I went to my aunt's house to make the phone call. By the time I returned, Dad had passed out and never knew I left the house. Although Dad would often show an affectionate side to the children of friends, we never saw that side of him. So often I feared my mother, brother, or I could have killed him. He pushed us that far.

I was so tired of our home life. It had been going on for years. I couldn't foresee it ever changing. I began to ask myself, "What is life all about?" I could see no purpose. I couldn't remember when I last felt happy. It had been years of fighting, fighting, and more fighting. There was no place to go to escape.

Feeling I couldn't cope with any more screaming, fighting, and anger and was unable to see anything beyond our miserable life, I decided I just didn't want to be here anymore. All of this was because of my father's need to drink. I felt certain life was never going to change.

Alone in my room, I took a razor and scratched my wrist. I

was sitting and looking at the scratch, preparing to do it again, except harder. Suddenly an unexplained peace took over my body.

A voice in my head said, "Don't do it. One day you will have children and a home."

It was so strange. I had never experienced anything like this before. It made me stop and think. I put the razor down and never contemplated anything like that again. I never forgot what happened; nor did I in any way connect what had just happened to God. After all, I didn't believe in Him.

CHAPTER 3

As I entered my senior year of high school, my relationship with my father hadn't changed one bit. Although I didn't lie, skip school, steal, smoke cigarettes, do drugs, drink, or have premarital sex, I was always in trouble. My sin was that I hated my father and I wasn't capable of hiding it from him. I had finally reached the point where I just wouldn't make eye contact with my father. In fact, I tried to stay out of his space altogether.

It bothered me that I hated him. I worried he would die and I'd have to live with the fact I hated him so much. I would never be able to make things right between us. Our relationship wasn't the way I wanted it, but I just couldn't help how I felt. But my fear didn't change my feelings. They were that deep. How could I pretend I loved and respected someone whom I so much despised?

I had watched my father mistreat my mother for years. I would never understand why she stayed, except she couldn't afford to leave him. And I was certain she would not have left her children with him. Did she really love him? How could she?

Halfway through my senior year, my next-door neighbor told me her nephew had seen my senior picture. He wanted her to arrange a date. Although I had never met her nephew, I remembered watching him play basketball when I was a freshman. A senior at the time, he was on the varsity basketball team. I knew he was also very good at football. I remembered watching him and only him as he played basketball and thinking how cute I thought he was. I was really flattered he would be interested in taking me out.

When I met Dick, he was recuperating from a work-related injury. He had serious surgery on his knee, and while so many guys his age were being drafted into the service, this would keep him from entering the service.

Once Dick and I began dating, I never went out with anyone else. I was still interested in a couple of other guys, but when told we were through if I dated anyone else, I didn't test him. Years later, as I looked back over my life, I would believe this was a mistake on my part. He now knew he could control me somewhat.

We had been dating for some time. We were watching television one evening when my father came home. Dad, as usual, had been drinking and was stumbling and slurring his words. Suddenly I was being sent to my room. This time I didn't even remember what upset him. Whatever it was, I didn't feel I had done anything that deserved being sent to my room. I was eighteen years old and would be graduating soon.

I couldn't believe my father acted like he did, and I was even more surprised when Dick said nothing. He just got up and left for home. I was as disappointed in Dick as I was angry at my father. At the time, I told myself that Dick didn't come to my defense because he didn't want to create a scene with my father. I failed to see to whom I was making a lifelong commitment.

Not long after I graduated from high school, while I was relaxing at home, the phone rang. Mom and Dad were, as they often were, at Lake Erie. It was my younger sister Carol. She had gone away with her boyfriend, who had just graduated with me.

She proudly announced, "Chuck and I just got married."

My response was, "You idiot! What did you do that for?"

Although I was certain Carol loved Chuck, I was also certain Carol had found an out, and Chuck was it. Living at our house was not fun. She had done something I would never have dreamed of going through with. Carol hadn't yet finished high school. But to her credit, even though she was married, she would finish school. The marriage, however, did not last. Many years later, I would discover Carol was as addicted to alcohol as our father was. It is something with which she would struggle her entire life.

About this time, my father's sister revealed to us that we had a sister. Unknown to us, our father had a wife before our mother. He had abandoned that family and come to Ohio, where he would eventually meet and marry my mother.

It seems a girl convinced my grandparents she was pregnant with my father's baby. Doing the proper thing, my grandparents made my father marry the girl, only to find she wasn't pregnant at the time. But she did become pregnant soon after the marriage. Although that doesn't excuse my father for his bad choices, I was beginning to understand why my father was so troubled. He definitely had to feel he had been wronged.

My father had come to Ohio and worked on my grandfather's farm, which was how he met my mother. My father married my mother when she became pregnant. Was this why he called my mother some of the names he did? Did he feel he had been trapped again? Did he not want to have children? Was this why he seemed angry all the time? Understanding life had not been good to him, I am far from forgiving him, but I am trying. After all, he had done it all to himself.

Most of what I learned about my parents would come from my aunt. My parents didn't talk about their lives. I knew very little about their lives before they became parents. Although they didn't talk about their past, neither did they voice their complaints about one another to us. Of course, they didn't really have to. We were witness to much of their discord. But to their credit, even though they fought constantly, neither would verbalize any complaints about their health or their lives. The fights were most always about my father's drinking and money.

After I graduated from high school, I took a job as a secretary at a small company downtown. I would eventually lose touch with my high school friends, and my world now revolved around the girls with whom I worked and my future husband. By this time, Dick and I had decided we would get married one day.

Wanting to get off to a good start, we saved everything we could. We would pay for most of our wedding ourselves. Dick came from a large family, which included three sisters and three brothers. His mother was a widow. Neither his mother nor my parents had the money for multiple weddings.

Three weeks before our wedding, Dick and I went to a Christmas dance. After a pleasant evening, where Dick obviously had too much to drink, we walked to our car. While waiting for the rest of our group to reach their cars, Dick passed out behind the wheel. Thank goodness we hadn't left the parking lot. One of the other guys moved Dick out of the driver's seat, and I drove to his house.

The next day, totally upset with the previous evening, I told him, "If you are going to drink, don't marry me." I never meant anything more in my life. There was no way on this earth I was going to follow in my mother's footsteps and be married to an alcoholic.

After that, for the most part, Dick would seldom drink more than he could hold. Everyone will slip occasionally. While I kept him from drinking too much, he kept me from beginning to smoke. Although he smoked, he absolutely hated to see a woman with a cigarette in her mouth. This kept me from picking up the habit.

A couple weeks later, on a terrible snowy day in January, we were married. Being two naïve young people, totally oblivious to the weather reports, the next morning we left for Washington, DC, a terrible choice for January. While on the way, our car heater would quit working. It was freezing and snowing.

Upon reaching our destination, we inquired about having our heater repaired. We found we couldn't afford to have the heater checked, let alone repaired.

After a couple days of freezing temperatures, we left Washington, DC, and headed to my grandparents' home in Pennsylvania. Once there, they directed us to a garage, where we could afford to have our heater repaired.

The funniest event on my honeymoon occurred at my grandparents' home. We were spending the night there. Exhausted from our day's travel, Dick and I had gone upstairs to bed before my grandparents. Unable to get to sleep, we decided we were used to sleeping on the opposite side of the bed.

As we were in the process of crawling over one another to change sides of the bed, my grandparents came up the stairs. This wasn't a box spring type bed. It was the old actual spring-style bed. I don't think I ever heard a bed squeak as loud as the bed we were in that night. To this day, this makes me laugh because I know what my grandmother thought was going on. I never did tell my grandmother what we were actually doing.

After our honeymoon, I returned to work. A few weeks later, I began feeling nauseous. My working career would be short-lived. Since I was newly married, having children hadn't even entered my mind. Before I had time to think about whether I wanted to be a mother, I would become one. Our first girl was born at the end of October.

When my first baby girl was born, I thought she was the

cutest baby I'd ever seen. She was adorable. But as I would jokingly say for years and years afterward, she came out of the womb with a mind of her own. If I said "don't do it," it was as though that was all she could think of doing. She would prove to be a challenge for me until she married and left my care.

When we had her baptized, the monsignor didn't like the way I spelled my daughter's name. We had named her Kristina Lynn. He informed me that was not a Christian spelling. I made no attempt to change the spelling of my daughter's name. I had only been a Catholic for a very short time. Since I had not grown up in the Catholic faith, his words irritated me.

After becoming pregnant so easily and quickly, I would ask myself, "Why am I a Catholic?" I believe in birth control. This, along with listening to the monsignor speak about money every Sunday, I was beginning to believe I was in the wrong church. Besides, I was not really sure I believed in God.

Our daughter was barely walking when we decided to build. We bought a lot from Dick's uncle, and with the help of many good friends, we built our first home. No longer doing office work, I thoroughly enjoyed building our home. I would run for supplies, clean up after the workers, assist with the electrical work, pound nails when necessary, and do all the painting, inside and out. It was much more fun than office work. And this felt like the right thing to do. I loved being free to work on my own schedule. Because I didn't have anyone to look after our daughter as I worked on our house, she would be with me all the time.

Two and a half years after the first baby, we had our second daughter. When my first was born, I knew nothing about being a mother. I knew I had made mistakes in raising my first and welcomed the challenge of doing better the second time. And our second child was an angel. She was perfect. She was always pleasant and happy, and unlike her older sister, she never cried.

She was a shy little girl, but so precious. We named her Tina Marie. I loved being a mother and had no desire to ever return to the work world. Raising children is work, but I enjoyed the challenge. I felt I was born to be a mother.

The new baby was only a few weeks old when Kris said something to me one day as I was washing dishes in the kitchen. As I turned to look at her, I couldn't believe my eyes. What was she doing? She was not yet three years old, and she was carrying her baby sister. Shocked and not believing she had done this, I didn't say a word. I didn't want to scare Kris. As quickly as I could, I dashed toward her to retrieve the baby.

This would only be the beginning. Kris would require my constant attention most of her childhood. It was not until she was no longer living with us that I could look back at the many memorable moments Kris gave me and appreciate her unique personality. She was an experience I couldn't have survived more than once.

Although my sisters and I have moved out of our family residence, my mother and brother were still home with my father. Things had not improved. In fact, since I had left, my father had been in a couple of bar brawls. Each time he received a black eye, which swelled tremendously. At this time my father would go to the local fishery, purchase a leech, and place it on his face to suck out the excess blood and reduce the swelling. I couldn't look at him when he did this without quivering.

I worried constantly about my mother and her safety. The years of stress were now written all over her face. She was very thin and ill much of the time, but she continued to work. A few times, needing a place to get away, Mom had come and stayed with us for a day or two. Then she would return home. I so wished she would have left my father permanently. Their relationship was so unhealthy. She deserved so much better.

When my mother stayed at my house, I worried my father

would come over looking for her. When he was drinking and angry, I was afraid of him. I never knew what he was capable of doing.

When I tried to talk with my husband about my parents, Dick informed me, "I don't want to hear anything about your parents' problems."

His attitude surprised and disappointed me. I would again think about how he had acted years earlier when my father sent me to my room and he had left abruptly. I was beginning to wonder if I had married the wrong person. I believed two married people should know what the other is thinking and feeling. He was supposed to be my best friend, and I couldn't talk to him. This side of him would never change. I realized he really didn't know or care what I was feeling. And for me, this would forever be a wedge between us.

Although Mom and Dad still fought constantly all week, they would also continue to go to Lake Erie as often as they could. By this time, they had graduated from putting up tents to leasing a cabin, and eventually my father had purchased a lot about a quarter mile from the lake and proceeded to build a rather nice cabin, mostly from secondhand materials brought from home. I would never understand how Mom and Dad could fight so much during the week and go to the lake for the weekend, acting like everything was normal. To me, it just never made any sense.

Never one to sit still, while Dick worked all day, I watched our children, mowed the lawn, kept our vehicles clean and polished, and did most of the work the husbands usually do around the house. I didn't mind. I loved doing the work. And this would leave his evenings free to help other friends with their homes, which he often did. I was okay with this, as our friends had helped us.

And because he was gone much of the time, as much as I

loved being a mother, there was never a day the girls weren't my responsibility. My husband was a hunter. Every hunting season, he had only one thing on his mind, to head out as often as he could. I looked at this as his vacation. I, on the other hand, would never get a day away from the kids. Dick would never understand that I could also use a break. Because I didn't have a job outside the home, he believed I never did anything. He said every day of my life was a vacation. He didn't believe in taking a vacation. Things hadn't changed since my childhood.

My vacations would still be the weekend. Dick and I would occasionally go to the cabin and visit my parents. If we went to the lake to visit, something always needed to be done around my parents' second home. We would spend our weekend helping them catch up. Again, just as when I was a child, we wouldn't be on the lake.

After seven years in our first home, I became restless to move again. When I suggested building once more, the thought would upset Dick. Any kind of change would always upset Dick. He didn't ever want anything to change. But with a little persistence and after pointing out the financial benefit, we would build our second home. To me, it was fun building because we were doing it together.

We had nearly finished the second house and moved in. We still had things to complete, but at least the house was livable. Dick was working outside, using a pick to dig a drainage line for the downspouts.

The girls were outside with him. He specifically told them, "Don't walk behind me." The words were no more out of his mouth, and Kris, now about eight years old, being her usual self, did not listen.

Just as he swung the pick, she walked behind him. Unable to stop his swing, he hit her on the top of the head with the tip of the pick. Her head was cut and bleeding, but fortunately, it wasn't a deep cut Knowing she needed to be checked, Dick would be too shook up to accompany us to the hospital. He sent us alone. So Kris and I would drive to the hospital. Upon arriving at the hospital, I would receive the third degree from the hospital staff.

I explained, "My husband hit her in the top of her head with a pick." To make matters worse, this was not Kris's first visit to the hospital.

When Kris was about four, the neighbor was upset with me because I couldn't keep my daughter at home. I had spanked her and told her to stay on the back patio. Never one to like being disciplined, Kris held her breath until she passed out. This time, she went into convulsions.

Not knowing what else to do, I picked her up and ran to the very same neighbor. We worked to get her to come to, after which I took her to the hospital. Kris would be hospitalized for a couple days while they ran tests on her.

When Dick and I visited, she had been put into a crib with a net on top. She wouldn't stay in her crib, so they had attached the net. She didn't heed to the nurses any better than she listened to me. As we walked into her hospital room, she had her hands on the crib bars and was pounding her head on the bars as hard as she could. As a result of that trip, she would be diagnosed as epileptic and would be on medication for a few years.

Now years later, here I was, bringing her back to the hospital with a bleeding head.

CHAPTER 4

My mother and father decided it was time to let go of our childhood home, as it was more space than they needed. While preparing to sell, my father was working on the lawn and burning weeds and leaves. A lot of smoke was coming from the fire, and the smoke would cover me. Unknown to me, poison ivy was in the fire.

A day after, I knew I was getting poison ivy. Even though no one could see it, I could feel it under my skin. I am very allergic to poison ivy. I have gotten poison ivy in the middle of winter after handling a calamine lotion bottle. So I made an appointment to see the doctor. I wanted him to give me a shot to counteract the poison ivy I knew I was going to get.

At his office, the doctor shared with me it was his first week practicing. The doctor looked at my clear arms, legs, and face and told me, "Go home, take a shower, and don't worry about it." He wouldn't give me a shot. I knew he thought I was crazy. Feeling disappointed, I went home.

Two days later, my hands were swelled up until I couldn't grip a comb to comb my hair. My eyes were tiny slits. I threw a wig on my head and again headed to the doctor. Unable to grip the steering wheel, I had to drive my car with the palms of my hands. Poison ivy now covered me everywhere, except under my panties and bra. Oozing and very swollen, I truly looked like something out of a horror movie.

As I arrived at the doctor's office, they didn't want me to sit in the waiting room. Someone escorted me immediately to the doctor's exam room. This time I would see the senior physician. After he looked at me, he called in the previous doctor to see me. As he entered the room, his eyebrows went up, and his jaw dropped. The look on his face is something I will never forget. My body was swelled so tight that it was hard for me to move. My skin was oozing. If the remedies the doctor gave me didn't work, he said I would have to be hospitalized.

At home, my mother would take the girls, and I would spend a few days in bed, wrapped in white strips of a bed sheet. With arms and legs unable to bend, I looked like a mummy. Since I had previously believed that doctors were always right, this would be my first wake-up moment, and I would realize they do make errors.

After years of feeling I did nothing but work, I found something I enjoyed more than anything I had ever done in my life. I began to play tennis. I never enjoyed anything as much as I enjoyed playing tennis. For me, it opened a whole new world.

Tennis was just beginning to become popular; thus at first there weren't a lot of places to play. At home in the basement, I would spend my time bouncing the ball off the wall, trying to speed up my reaction time. During the winter months, my friend and I would sweep the snow off the outdoor tennis court at a local apartment complex. We would use colored balls so we could find the balls in the snow. I was really hooked.

She and I would eventually sign up for lessons. There, I would meet someone who would become part of my life for many years. There was just something about the instructor's voice. I don't ever remember meeting someone and having the feeling I knew this person before. She had come from another state, so there was no way I had ever run into her before.

My tennis instructor also taught gymnastics, and Kris would become interested. As much as I loved tennis, Kris would love gymnastics. Because the gymnastics classes and indoor tennis courts were in the same facility, it worked out perfectly for us to both to enjoy our newfound hobbies. Tina would try gymnastics, but it wasn't her thing. An especially shy girl, she preferred to stay home. She wasn't outgoing like her older sister.

The cost of gymnastics and tennis would be a problem for my husband. Although I felt we could afford it, Dick didn't believe in spending money you didn't have to spend. He was still in the mode we were in when we were saving to get married. I guess he expected me to save every penny I could for the rest of my life. He would spend much of his time irritated with me because of money, and this part of him would never change.

We just didn't think alike. For example, once I reached my goal, I could loosen the strings and enjoy life. Dick would never share this feeling. Because he was extremely poor as a child, I can understand where he is coming from, but that was then, and this is now.

We had been in our second home only a few short years when I once again got the urge to move one last time. The developer of our allotment had opened a new street. There was a lot on top of a hill that I just loved.

Once again, I started begging my husband to build one more home. With this move, we would have our home paid off. We were young and healthy. Why not? It took a lot more begging than the first time, but I couldn't let go of the urge to build one last time. I felt this was something we really should do. This time, instead of doing most of the work ourselves, we could afford to subcontract more of the work. It would still be work, but not quite as much as the two previous homes had been. Dick reluctantly caved, and even though he didn't want to do it, we would build that third home.

Things didn't go as smoothly this time. There was a building boom at the time, and getting supplies was sometimes impossible. We couldn't get rock lathe to plaster. Then they were plastering the new house, and we still didn't have all the windows. We couldn't get plywood for the subfloor. It was one thing after another. Still I was not sorry we made the move. I knew I was where I wanted to be.

It was hard on Dick, but it was a good move for us. We had a much better lot and house. I have never been sorry we made that last move. I felt like I was home, and I would never suggest building again.

We had been living in our third home for a couple years when I first experienced the visions of which I previously spoke. Dick didn't listen to my rambling about my visions. I'm not sure he ever heard what I was saying. He worked and brought home the money. I paid the bills, cooked the meals, and cared for the kids. He didn't share his feelings and didn't ask about mine. We were like two strangers living together. At the same time, my daughter was still in gymnastics and doing very well. And I was still playing tennis. Both of these things also continued to anger my husband.

At this time, God came into my life. When I look back over my years on this planet, I can understand why He came into my life when He did. Things were going to change dramatically, and I was going to need Him. Once I found God, I began to look at everything in life in a different way. I would realize I had spent most of my life concentrating on myself and what I could do, mostly for myself. I realized there were things about myself I didn't like. I knew I could do better.

No longer thinking only of myself and wanting to do the right thing, I would begin my day asking God what I should do that day. Then I would do whatever it was I felt I was supposed to do. Years later, this would enable me to look back at the past without any regrets. I knew I was following God and this would keep me from ever having any regrets.

With the strain in our marriage, my husband and I were intimate only one time in a year when I became pregnant. It certainly wasn't something I had planned. I was as surprised as anyone. And when I told Dick we were having another baby, he was furious. Our daughters were twelve and nearly fifteen. He didn't want to start over. Once Dick found out we were having another child, the only time he spoke to me during my pregnancy was in the presence of others. It was cold war.

Because of my previous visions, I felt this baby was part of God's plan for us. And I am certain it was, except it would be many years before I would fully understand. Living with the stress brought on by my visions and the lack of communication with my husband, by the time the baby was born, I was ready to divorce my husband and told him so.

Knowing I was not too happy with my marriage, a friend had asked me, "Why do you stay married?"

Because I was asking God every day what I should do, I would realize divorce was not part of God's plan for me. That was not what I was being told to do. With the birth of our third daughter, the stress I felt because of the fear of losing my friend disappeared. I didn't know what God was telling me, but I had to let it go.

Confronted with the realization I'd just about had it with him, Dick would change somewhat. He named the new baby and took an interest in her that he had never shown his first two daughters. For the first time, he became involved and more of a father.

We named our new daughter, Melanie Ann. She was probably the only reason our marriage didn't fall apart. Her sisters, father, and I all adored her. When it came to being good, she even surpassed her sister Tina.

With the help of two sisters, she advanced quickly, and she was walking by nine months. Being a mother for the third time is much easier when you have two teenagers to help with the baby. Her sisters enjoyed her, and I don't think they minded helping.

Unable to forget how their father treated me during the pregnancy, I couldn't let go of my disgust with him. This would prove to be another wedge I wasn't sure I would ever get past. We didn't verbally argue, but a definite distance was between us. It had been years, and he was still pouting about making the third move. Feeling we had done the right thing, I was content in my new environment. I knew I wasn't going to want to move again.

While I was dealing with my small problems, both of my sisters were dealing with their own issues. Carol, who was now living out West, would get breast cancer and have a breast removed. Soon after, she would meet someone new, fall in love, and marry for a second time. My older sister Pat was now married with two small children. Pat would be diagnosed with a cancerous brain tumor. At least it was operable. Pat would have her head shaved and endure brain surgery.

The first time I saw my sister after her surgery, she was in the intensive care unit. Not comfortable with the hospital setting, as I walked into the room, I had never before seen anyone hooked to so many tubes and machines. Her condition shocked me. I felt terrible for her. She looked so weak and fragile.

As I walked across the room to visit, I began to faint. As a paramedic, my brother-in-law was familiar with stressful situations. He obviously recognized the look on my face. I will never know how he crossed that room so quickly and caught me before I hit the floor. Although I felt great sorrow for my sister, I really didn't know what to say, except I was sorry she had to endure this.

Years earlier, shortly after her marriage, Pat had lost her firstborn. She was in the final week of her pregnancy when the baby's umbilical cord wrapped around her neck, and the baby was strangled in the womb. It seemed life was always harder for my older sister.

Melanie was a little over one year old when Kris, Melanie, and I were headed to the store one evening. As I walked to the garage, Dick was outside, talking with his cousin Larry and Larry's next-door neighbor. They had stopped by to visit.

I knew Larry before I met Dick. He too was a cousin to my old next-door neighbors. Years earlier, I had a crush on Larry. I don't think I was ever around Larry when he didn't have a smile on his face. He always seemed to enjoy life. He was a happy, fun-loving guy.

After speaking with them for a few moments, we left and headed to the store. As we were returning home a short time later, we would be the last car to come down the street before the police closed the road. There had been an accident. They weren't letting any more vehicles through. We had no choice but to pull off the road and wait.

As we waited, a paramedic walked past our car. He stated a motorbike had hit a pothole. The bike upset, and the rider's head had hit the bumper of the oncoming car. His brains were all over the road. For some unknown reason, I had a sick feeling that the accident involved Larry.

After I got home, I called another of Dick's cousins and told her there was an accident. I wasn't sure, but I had a feeling it was Larry. I hadn't thought about my vision for quite some time. Could this be what God had warned me about?

I told her, "I think this is the accident I felt a few years earlier when I had my first vision."

I would soon find out it was Larry. Days after his death, my mind would once again begin to wonder, "What exactly was God trying to tell me? Why can't I let go of the other vision?" I now felt certain they must be two separate events.

Sometime after Larry's death, I remembered my own mother had told me that Larry's mother kept going over to the house of her sister, my old next-door neighbor, crying. She believed Larry was going to be killed on his motorcycle. I hadn't thought about this for years. We don't remember these things because you don't believe they will happen at the time you hear them. It is something I probably would never have recalled, except it did happen. Larry's mother had been right.

Larry's mother would be the only person I ever knew who perhaps could have given me some sort of answer to my visions. Although I knew her, I didn't feel I knew her well enough to approach her about such a sensitive subject.

After she passed, I would forever regret I didn't ask her how she knew.

CHAPTER 5

One afternoon, Dick, Melanie, and I were sitting on our front porch. Melanie was about two and a half years old. The neighbor kids were playing on our front lawn. We were watching them as they played games and were having a good time.

Distracted, we were unaware Melanie had wandered next door to our neighbors. She couldn't have been gone more than a few minutes. Our neighbors had just installed an in-ground pool and hadn't yet put up a fence.

My neighbor heard something and looked out his upstairs bedroom window. Our toddler was at the steps to his pool. Thank God our neighbor heard her. Melanie had wandered off so quickly and quietly that we hadn't yet missed her.

Melanie had no fear of water. I had taken her to early swimming classes, so she was familiar with water. But she certainly wouldn't have been able to save herself, had she fallen in. We were so fortunate that it was not her time to leave us. Not everyone is as fortunate as we were. When it happens to you, you realize how quickly something like this can happen. You learn not to judge.

Shortly thereafter, our neighbors erected a fence. They let us know we were welcome to use the pool. As I loved to swim, I think we became part of their family. I had always wanted a pool, but as Dick didn't swim, he could have cared less. Sometimes I feel we should not have been at their house as often as we were, but they always made us feel welcome and encouraged us to come back.

As I loved water almost as much as I loved tennis, I would begin to go swimming instead of playing tennis. And so my tennis years would dwindle.

My older girls were young ladies by now and working. They were growing up so fast. I was glad I still had another young one to enjoy. I loved being a mother. As I grew and learned to understand my children, I enjoyed each one even more than the one before.

Because of the circumstances under which Melanie was born, I felt certain she was a gift from God. I knew I was supposed to have her. Melanie never needed reprimanded. She was always so good. I felt fortunate to have such a good child. I never needed to worry about her. She would be that way her entire life.

My oldest daughter would finish high school soon. She would attend summer school in order to have enough credits to graduate in three years. When she wanted to do something, nothing was going to stop her. She was ready to get on with her life.

By this time, I had decided the only way to get along with my oldest child was to stop being her mother and just become a friend. Born with a mind of her own, Kris had never welcomed advice from anyone, especially me. She was going to do her own thing in her own time.

When in a couple years she decided she was getting married, her father and I weren't very happy about it. We didn't care for her choice of husbands. We thought he had a drinking and drug problem, but Kris wouldn't see it.

It was only one week until the wedding. Tina and I had

planned a wedding shower for Kris at our house. While preparing for the shower, which would be the next day, we received a shocking phone call. Dick's mother had passed away unexpectedly.

The following week, instead of preparing for the wedding, we were getting ready for a funeral. Dick's mother would be buried in the dress she had purchased for the wedding. The death of his mother would send Dick into a mood that lasted for years. If I thought he had been unpleasant before, I would find it could get worse. His father had passed away before I knew Dick. I didn't know how he handled that time in his life.

When his family had to share his mother's small estate with her husband of a few years, Dick was livid. His mother had worked very hard all her life to raise seven children on her own. She was by no means well-to-do.

A few months after his mother's death, his stepfather, who was still living in his mother's house, fell down the basement steps at their home and passed away as well. His mother's small estate would now include his stepfather's children. It was all Dick could think and talk about. He was constantly in a foul mood. It was something of which he just could not let go.

After one short year of marriage, Kris realized she had made a mistake in her choice of husbands and got a divorce. Used to being on her own, she moved into an apartment after a brief stay with her father and me. Within months, she would soon fall in love with another tenant, Dan. She and Dan had been coworkers years earlier while in high school.

A few months later, Dan took her to Florida to meet his mother. Before they came home, I had the feeling they had gotten married. Kris was never one to confide in me, it was just something I felt. When they came home, my feelings proved to be correct. While visiting his mother, they had gotten married. It had been so sudden, but it would prove to be one of the best moves my daughter ever made. He would prove to be the perfect husband for my daughter. The second time around, she had chosen very wisely.

While our life had taken on a new direction, my sister Pat's life would also change, which unfortunately wouldn't be pleasant. Although I had always found it hard to get along with my sister, since her surgery, Pat had become hostile with most everyone.

I often wondered what her children might be going through. Living with their mother could not have been a pleasant experience. Although Pat's husband stood by her for years, he eventually decided he could no longer stay married to her. Many wouldn't understand his decision and criticized him, but our family would never speak harshly about her husband. People always gossip, but we knew he had done everything he could for her and saw to it she had what she needed. We knew he was a good person, but we all have our limits, and he had reached his. His marriage was definitely ruining his health. And with her husband out of the picture, it would put more of the responsibility of Pat's everyday care on our family. Although her children helped, they were young and couldn't be expected to handle all of their mother's needs.

By this time, my father was no longer working and spent most of his time sitting on his bed, leaning on his portable stand, breathing his oxygen, and watching television. Although Dad had emphysema, he continued to smoke and often would smoke with the oxygen at his nose. He was always quick to assure us this was safe. I think only he believed this.

His health has caused him to drink less, which made it easier for me to communicate with him. My feelings toward him were beginning to soften. I no longer hated him, but I didn't feel sorry for him either. As long as I could remember, Dad had not taken care of himself.

My mother was still working every day. I don't think she was looking forward to the day when she retired and would be trapped all day in their tiny house with her husband. My father continued to argue with her about most everything. Mom's hobby would be raising violets in the basement. It wasn't hurting a thing, but he would even complain about that.

At some point, he must have been upset about the number of clothes Mom had because she would no longer buy anything new to wear. It didn't matter if it were for a wedding, graduation, or holiday. She would not buy anything new. She didn't have that many clothes. Never in her life did she have an abundance of clothing. Again I would not be able to understand how or why she continued to live with him.

A lifetime of stress finally caught up with my mother. She never seemed to be feeling well anymore. Her illnesses were becoming more and more frequent and serious. She would be hospitalized for gall bladder surgery. Her next hospital stay would be because of a severe headache. Mom had a brain aneurism. Years after Pat's brain surgery, it was now Mom's turn to have a procedure.

Mom survived the surgery, only to have a stroke that night that left her paralyzed on her left side. She was unable to talk clearly and was partially paralyzed on her left side, but her speaking would eventually correct itself. In time, she regained enough movement to walk with a severe limp, but she never regained the use of her left arm. But Mom never complained. She took her disability in stride, but she would never be quite the same. She was so fragile.

Out of the blue, my father would receive a totally unexpected phone call from someone I am pretty certain he had not spent a lot of time thinking of in his lifetime, Nancy, the daughter he had abandoned when she was just a baby. Not long after the communication opened between the two of them, Nancy would come to visit her long-lost father.

When I first saw her, I thought she very much resembled my older sister. I felt badly for her since she had been abandoned, yet I thought she had no idea what life with her father would have been like. Nancy had the appearance of someone who had led a very rough life. She obviously didn't have a lot of money. I hate to say it, but I thought she looked as though she could have been into drugs, alcohol, or both. Believing this, I could not let myself get close to her. I liked her, but I already had all I could handle with our family. I didn't have the energy to give anyone else.

After a short visit, Nancy returned to Las Vegas. A few years later, she would once again visit. After the second visit, I didn't know if she and my father stayed in touch. I assume they did, but I don't really know.

Feeling I needed a break, I took a job at a local computer store. I felt as though I usually caught on to things pretty quickly, but I found I couldn't concentrate. What I was doing just didn't seem important to me. So when my employer was just about finished with my training, I quit. I felt bad about my decision, but my heart just wasn't into the job. The money wasn't that important, and there were more significant things in my life. I wanted to be available for my family.

Mom and Dad seldom left their home. Neither was doing very well. I was worried about both of them. Unable to stay in her home, Pat had been moved to an apartment. She needed someone to live with her. Pat had reached a point where she was no longer able to function without assistance. She had written checks and paid her bills. That was fine, but she overlooked making the deposit. All the checks bounced. It was becoming apparent that Pat was no longer capable of living alone. Even though I knew my sister needed someone to look after her, I wasn't able to invite my sister to live at my home. I knew that would be disastrous for everyone.

Years earlier, I had our small family over for Thanksgiving dinner. The day had gone extremely well until after dinner when we collected in the rec room downstairs. Melanie was bouncing a small ball. She wasn't being noisy. She was quietly entertaining herself with the ball. I guess the bouncing of the ball on the carpet must have upset my sister. For some totally unknown reason, Pat screamed at Melanie. No one had ever spoken to Melanie in that tone. We never had to discipline her. She was always so good. I didn't say anything to Pat, but once again, I wouldn't be able to understand my older sister. Things between us would never go smoothly.

Now alone, Pat needed a roommate. Carol, my younger sister who had been living in California, had once again divorced. After trying to start a small business on her own in California, she found she could no longer financially survive in California. Much to her dismay, Carol was left with no alternative but to return home. Mom and Dad sent her the money to get home. Thus, our dilemma with Pat was solved, and Carol found a home.

Carol was not happy about returning. She hated it here. I am certain she did not want to live with Pat. I was just happy she was returning. It would be nice to have someone to share in caring for our family. Life had become so hectic. It had been years and years since anyone hadn't needed help with something. It seemed someone always had a doctor's appointment or was in the hospital. It was a constant rotation of who was the most ill. I was beginning to feel overwhelmed. It seemed everyone was falling apart on me.

While Carol was sharing the apartment with Pat, Pat said one evening that someone was looking in the window at her. She was on the second floor. No one could have been looking in the window. Since she had changed significantly in her looks, I am certain Pat saw her reflection and no longer recognized her own image. Pat was having a hard time separating reality and hallucinations. My older sister once again reached a point where she had to be hospitalized. Her condition was worsening. While in the hospital, it was sometimes necessary for Pat to be fed intravenously.

After a couple days on the intravenous feeding, I noticed that Pat's personality would change. She was pleasant and made sense when she was talking. This had happened several times. If I had noticed this, did her doctors? I believed Pat had serious vitamin and mineral deficiencies, which were being corrected when she was fed intravenously but not when she relied on regular meals.

Meanwhile my father was often upset with the number of doctor appointments my mother had. He would make cruel comments to Mom. He felt the doctors were just after money and running unnecessary tests. It was my understanding that my father, in not too pleasant terms, expressed his feelings to the doctors. He was never one to keep his opinions to himself.

Unfortunately Pat had the same doctors. Although the doctors didn't drop my mother as a patient, they withdrew from Pat's case, leaving my sister without a doctor. Pat was now in the hospital without a regular doctor to look after her needs. She was in the hands of whichever intern was on call at the time.

On one icy winter night, I had driven Pat's two children to the hospital to visit with her. Soon after I entered the room, she snapped at me, telling me not to touch her. I withdrew from her bedside. I knew she didn't feel well, and if she felt up to visiting with anyone, it would have been her children.

This would be the last time I saw my sister. Shortly thereafter, early in the morning without any family present,

Pat would pass away. Since the hospital did not really know what caused her death, an autopsy was performed. Weeks later, my mother told me that Pat had died of an accidental, intern-administered drug overdose.

CHAPTER 6

The summer after Pat passed away, Dick and I would begin traveling with our youngest daughter. Melanie had proved to be very athletic. She was only ten years old when she was invited to play on a softball team with girls older than herself.

And this would only be the beginning. Every summer through high school, we would be traveling with our daughter while she played softball. Melanie was fortunate to be playing with teams who would usually qualify for large tournaments at the end of the season, which would require traveling outside our local area. For me, this meant a vacation.

Traveling with Melanie and her teammates would be the first vacations I would ever enjoy. In addition to the trips within our home state, we would visit Oklahoma, Texas, Alabama, and North Carolina. There was never time to sightsee. Seventy-five percent of our time was spent watching softball games.

For years, my life had pretty much consisted of taking someone to an appointment or running after something someone needed. It was nice to be with someone who was not ill. It was relaxing to get out of my routine and be around others. We would meet a lot of very nice people during this time. It was something positive to think about, which I very much needed. It was also something that helped me to keep my sanity.

Because of the visions I had experienced years earlier, I was now a firm believer in reincarnation. To me, this only made sense. I believe we are born over and over again. Each lifetime we learn a new lesson, and ultimately our soul becomes worthy of entering heaven. With all of our earthly faults, if each of us went to heaven when we died, wouldn't heaven soon become just like earth?

Within one year after her second marriage, Kris became pregnant. I believed perhaps the baby she was carrying was my older sister's soul. Although not positive, this would be something I felt very strongly. It had been a year and half since Pat had passed away.

It was the day before Thanksgiving. I had been cleaning and preparing for the dinner we would be having at our house the next day. Dick's family was going to be here. We were expecting about fifty people. Each family was going to bring a dish, so I didn't have to prepare a lot of things. It was just a matter of getting organized. I was never one to wait until the last minute to do things. I'm usually prepared for the unexpected. I was finished and ready to relax for the evening.

The phone rang. It was my mother. She felt she needed to go to the hospital. She just didn't feel right. I picked her up, and we headed to the emergency room. After examining her, they couldn't find any problem and were prepared to send her out the door. But suddenly everything went crazy. Mom was rushed back into the emergency room. At night's end, she was on life support. I was at the hospital until very late that evening. The next morning, I let my sister and brother tend to my mother. I needed to be home, at least for part of the day. I would see my mother that night.

At the hospital, my mother kept unhooking her tubes. It became necessary to tie down her arms. When I saw her that evening, she looked so uncomfortable. She wasn't able to speak;

nor was she capable of writing legibly. But she obviously was not happy about her condition.

After a few days, believing my mother would not survive without life support, the doctors needed permission to disconnect her. My father would have to make this decision. But days passed, and he was having a terrible time struggling with that choice. He wasn't handling the situation very well. He looked tired and exhausted, but he would eventually sign the necessary papers.

After Pat's passing, Carol had moved into an apartment next door to our parents. When Carol stopped in after work, she found Dad passed out on the floor. Dad must have had a premonition because he had instructed Carol that under no circumstances were she to call an ambulance for him. Shocked at his condition, Carol forgot what he had told her and immediately called for the paramedics.

Dad was taken to the hospital and placed in intensive care. My mother had now been taken off life support and survived. Both would be in intensive care. And when it was time for my parents to be released from the intensive care unit to a step-down room, I stopped by the nurse's desk and left a message. I told them, "They don't get along. Please don't put them into the same room." I then left for the day.

The next morning I would find my request had been ignored. They put my parents into the same room, and as usual, they got into an argument. Neither was very strong. Still they could find the energy to exchange hostilities.

After words with my mother, my father was angry and decided he was leaving the hospital. When he didn't have any clothes and the staff wouldn't provide them, he was going to leave without the clothes. Of course the hospital staff was not going to let that happen. My father was admitted to the psychiatric ward. Had they known my father was used to getting his own way, they would have known treating him in this manner was not going to end well.

For years, my father had spent most of his time in an upright position. It enabled him to breathe with less effort. The last time I saw my father, he was constrained and unable to speak clearly. Did he have a stroke, or was he drugged? I had no idea what was going on with my father.

Shortly thereafter, my dad passed away in the psychiatric ward, somewhere I truly believe he did not belong. My father always had a short fuse, and while it was not easy for me to get along with him, I didn't for one second think he was in a state of mind that required being locked in a psychiatric ward. Just as when Pat had passed away, just too many things were happening too quickly. There wasn't time to ask questions. There was always something or someone else who needed my attention.

Weeks earlier, on Thanksgiving Day, we had been prepared to lose our mother. Instead it was one week before Christmas, and we were burying our father. And once my father passed away, my mother never once spoke about him. She didn't even want to hear anything about his funeral. After all these years of abuse, my mother was emotionally finished with my father.

Strangely, the summer before my father passed away, he and I were talking. Kris was pregnant for the second time.

I mentioned to my father, "I think you are going to be reborn to Kris."

My father looked at me and gave me the most pleasant smile I think he had ever given me in his life.

The spring after my father passed away, Kris would give birth to a baby boy on Good Friday. I truly felt this was a message from God.

When Mom left the hospital, she went to a nursing home. When they felt perhaps she could leave, we tried everything.

She stayed at my house for a short time. I was not qualified to handle Mom's needs. We hired someone to come into her house to assist her. We bought an intercom so my sister, who was next door, would know if she needed something.

But nothing worked. Mom needed more intensive care than could be provided at home, and once again, she would go back to the nursing home. I believe my mother was sent from the hospital, home, or nursing home seven times in the past year. She was apparently never going to lead a self-sufficient life again. She was always going to need assistance.

With Dad gone and Mom never being able to live in her home again, I was left with the job of disposing of their home and its contents. Since they were heavy smokers, most everything in their home was unusable. My sister and brother smoked, so they took what they wanted. The rest was mostly thrown away. After clearing out the house, I cleaned it as well as I could. I could never get rid of the smoke smell. I listed the house for sale. Their house qualified for a government-assisted loan for the purchaser.

Not knowing how the system worked, I listed with a realtor. Unknown to me, once I had signed the papers, a licensed professional needed to make all future repairs to the home. Although my husband and I had built three homes and my brother's occupation was repairing and remodeling homes, we had to pay someone to make all necessary changes or repairs.

This was my first stupid mistake. I then replaced the smelly carpet and added new wallpaper to the bath and kitchen areas of the house. It was a small house, so it didn't require a large amount of carpet or wallpaper, but it was still a foolish thing for me to do after I had already listed the house.

In addition to the extra burden of disposing of their home and its contents, I had a two-inch-high pile of doctor and hospital bills that required my attention. Besides Medicare,

Mom and Dad each had insurance with a different company. At that time, the healthcare system wasn't streamlined as it is today. It was necessary to make copies of everything, send each bill to the correct insurance company, and pay the correct amount. It was very confusing and time consuming.

After numerous roommates, my mother would share her room with a woman we all adored. She too would become a part of our family. When we visited our mother, all of us visited. I was glad Mom had a friend with whom she could spend the long days.

We had been called to the nursing home several times lately. Mom wasn't doing very well. Late one evening, I received a phone call from the nursing home. This time they wanted me to keep my mother company because her roommate had passed away. I stayed that evening until I felt comfortable about leaving. When I left my mother, I mentioned to her that Kris, the babies, and I would be in the next day to visit.

That night, as I talked to God about the day's events, I realized for the past year that my mother no longer wanted to be here. She had told me that. I realized I was the one holding my mother here. She was ready to leave, but I hadn't been ready to let her go. I said to God, "I don't want to see my mother suffer anymore."

The next day, about noon, Kris, her two children, and I entered my mother's room. Mom was lying in her bed and looked at us as we entered.

I said hi to her and then said to Courtney, "Come see Grandma."

As I reached for Courtney, my mother immediately shook her head no. She didn't say anything. She just closed her eyes, and she was gone. She knew we were coming, and I know she waited for us to get there.

Although each had been sick for a very long time, in four

short years, I had lost half of my childhood family. To say the least, I was exhausted. It had been years since I felt as though I could sit down and actually relax. It had been a long road, lasting many years, and now it was over.

My mother had filled so much of my time over the years that I considered her my best friend. I had lost contact with my school friends, the girls with whom I had worked, and my tennis buddies. At least my sister Carol was here. Carol would now become my closest friend and confidant.

CHAPTER 7

would recall a conversation I had with my mother years earlier. We were discussing my new relationship with God. I wished I could make my mother understand the peace that could come with communicating with God.

At the time, my mother informed me that she didn't believe in God. She told me, "I am an atheist. Life on earth is hell." Although my mother hadn't been to church for many years, she had been brought up in the Catholic faith. I was surprised to hear she didn't believe in God. By this time, I too believed life on earth was hell, but at the same time, I also believed life on earth could be heaven. I believe it all depended upon where we were in our spiritual growth.

It seemed everyone in my family was going through some sort of despair. Other than the anguish I felt for them, my life hadn't been that bad. I felt I had been very fortunate. Most of all, I had my health, which I thank God for all the time. At the time, I truly believed the bad years were behind me. I was looking forward to life without stress. But that would prove to be a fantasy. The peace I had hoped would fill my life after the deaths of my sister and parents just wasn't about to happen.

I would try several different jobs. I wasn't content with any of them and didn't stick with it for very long. I felt I needed a refresher course. Computers were now the way to do things.

I was taking adult training classes so I might freshen up my typing and accounting skills. I was at the class when I received an emergency phone call.

My husband had a doctor's appointment, which ended up with him going immediately to the hospital. At the hospital, it was decided he needed emergency heart surgery. They felt he should go to a larger hospital about an hour away. Thus, that same night, he was transferred to the bigger facility. They would do the surgery first thing the next morning.

At the hospital, they had hoped that stents would be sufficient to clear the blockages he had in his arteries. But after hours of surgery and not seeing the desired results, he would go directly into open heart surgery. It would be more than twelve hours before we were notified they had finished his surgery.

Prior to his operation, Dick had been working out of the area and had been gone all week. He was sleeping on a garage floor in the southern part of the state. He had changed employers and was earning half what he previously brought home. Although we didn't have a mortgage, we still had utilities, groceries, taxes, insurance, and so on. And because Dick never had any responsibility handling our household expenses, he had no idea what amount was needed to just make ends meet. Had I not gone back to work, we would not have been able to pay our bills. I had asked him to change jobs, but he ignored me. He was going to do what he wanted to do.

Dick had been carrying his anger about his mother's estate for quite a long time. It had been years since we last moved, but he was still resentful toward me about it. He could really carry a grudge. I truly believe this combination of events was why he had a problem. Your blood doesn't flow as it should when you are constantly carrying anger in your body. It just isn't healthy. After surgery, Dick was going to be off work for some time. He needed time to think about life, and this would be a good time for him to do it.

While Dick had his problems with his health, my middle daughter was also having issues. Tina had been displaying some erratic behavior for some time. I didn't understand. Perhaps all the family stress was getting to her as well. Tina had always been a very sensitive girl.

The first time I noticed she was behaving differently, she had been living with her high school sweetheart, to whom she was engaged. When that relationship didn't work out, she had moved home. It was then I really noticed how much she had changed. As time passed, she would have periods when she seemed perfectly normal. Then suddenly she would say or do something that made no sense. We were concerned, but no one specific event said she definitely had a problem.

When Tina met someone and fell in love for the second time, she once again became engaged. I am certain she never cared about anyone as much as she cared for John. She was crazy about him. Unfortunately in time, this relationship also would end.

After the second breakup, I believe Tina was depressed for quite some time. Something was happening to her. As the years passed, it was becoming increasingly harder to understand what was going on in her mind.

Tina had a warm and loving personality. She would make a good impression when she applied for a job. But once she had the job, the stress of working regular hours and the responsibility of the position would take its toll. She would mentally lose control of her life and end up getting fired. It was happening over and over again.

Although we were aware something was wrong with Tina, as she was now considered an adult, we didn't know what to do or how to go about getting her help. When I tried to talk with her about seeing someone, she wasn't going to have anything to do with that.

I had never had any problem getting along with Tina. She had always been a pleasant daughter. We had always been close, but to her, I had become her enemy, and I had no idea why. In her mind, I was the one who needed to see a doctor. There was nothing wrong with her.

On one occasion, she accused me of spilling a drink in her car. I had no idea what she could be talking about. I hadn't been near her car. Next, she accused me of sticking pins into a voodoo doll, causing her pain. This made absolutely no sense to me. I had never heard of such a thing. Where did these thoughts come from? Was it from the strange movies she watched while living with her first boyfriend? I had no idea. Her life was getting more and more bizarre. Eventually Tina would physically attack me, stating she wanted to kill me. I was at a loss. I had no idea what was going on in her mind. Somehow in Tina's thinking, I was behind all of her problems.

When Tina's current boss called me concerning Tina, he said he felt bad, but he had to let her go. Tina believed someone was sending messages to her through her computer. He felt she needed to see someone.

When I couldn't convince Tina she needed help, she went to visit her older sister. She was confused and making no sense whatsoever at the time. Somehow Kris convinced her to go with her to talk with a minister. And as the minister talked with Tina, he suggested she be taken to the crisis center. Surprisingly Tina agreed to go.

The visit to the crisis center ended up with Tina being admitted to a behavioral hospital. After a few days, she was diagnosed as paranoid schizophrenic. After Tina left the hospital, she had a caseworker who contacted her regularly to see if she were taking her medication and doing okay. Tina would forever declare she didn't need medicine. The medication helped somewhat, but by no means cured her.

Even though we now had a diagnosis, I really couldn't understand what was happening to my beautiful daughter. I knew nothing about schizophrenia. Unable to understand Tina's illness, most of her friends had disappeared. She was becoming increasingly isolated from the real world.

Melanie was in the final year of high school when she went to see an orthodontist about the slight overlap of her upper front teeth. Believing it shouldn't be too much of a problem to correct, the orthodontist said he could correct her bite in one year. That sounded reasonable, so we made arrangements to have the braces applied. What could possibly go wrong?

As we neared the end of the year, I received a letter from the orthodontist. When I read it, I was never more upset with anyone in my life. I could not believe what I was reading. He stated Melanie was going to have a problem with her jaw. He recommended she have surgery to break her jaw and reset it. I thought, *you have got to be kidding. Break my daughter's jaw and reset it? Why?* I was so angry that I could not even talk to the orthodontist. I didn't ever want to set eyes on him again.

Melanie had no problem with her jaw before he worked on her teeth. Now I was supposed to go along with letting someone break my daughter's jaw and reset it. I just couldn't let go of my anger and total disgust with this orthodontist. I had never contacted a lawyer before in my life. I didn't think I would ever consider suing anyone. But this time, I could not accept what he had done to my daughter.

I contacted several lawyers, all to no avail. Even though all I wanted was my money returned, no one would even consider representing me. One lawyer stated he wouldn't take a case that represented less than $50,000.

Having already paid for what was supposed to be an easy

fix, I only wanted someone else to correct my daughter's bite, and I certainly didn't think I should have to be the one to pay for it. Although I never repeated anything derogatory to anyone about the dentist, I had sent a letter to the local paper regarding my predicament. The letter was printed. I didn't name the orthodontist.

Shortly thereafter, I received a letter from a lawyer representing the orthodontist. The lawyer stated I was defaming the orthodontist and he was considering suing me. What a joke! No one would represent me, but he had no problem finding someone to represent him.

I sent a copy of the orthodontist's letter to the lawyer. I asked him, "Would you let him work on your children's teeth?" I also stated he should tell the orthodontist to sue me. I told him, "I want to be heard. I haven't said anything that isn't true, and the first thing I will do is call the local paper and tell them he is suing me."

I never heard from the lawyer again. After contacting numerous people regarding my complaint, after nearly one year, I realized I was fighting a losing battle. No one was going to help me. Melanie would eventually see another orthodontist, have two teeth pulled, and once again endure another year of braces. Just as suspected, it was not necessary to break her jaw.

It would take me years to forgive that orthodontist, but in time, I realized he was human and had made a huge error in judgment. I let go of my anger.

CHAPTER 8

After both of our parents were gone, as much as my sister hating living in our hometown, Carol decided to purchase a duplex near the hospital, a very nice place with the upstairs being the second apartment. She felt the extra income would help her make the payments. She had moved in and was getting her life organized.

At the same time I was upset with Melanie's orthodontist, Carol had a routine dental cleaning. A smoker, she was having problems with her gums. The day after the cleaning, she became terribly ill. One day she was perfectly healthy; the next she was terribly ill. Days went by, and she wasn't getting any better. It had come on so quickly.

It became necessary for her to see a doctor. Upon seeing him, Carol would be told her kidneys were no longer functioning and she would need a kidney transplant. Without a new kidney, she would need dialysis to cleanse her body.

Knowing Carol needed a transplant, I felt I should offer one of mine. My body had not yet accepted the deaths of my sister and my parents. I was also terribly concerned about Tina. I just felt I couldn't risk having a problem with my own health right now. Feeling I needed more time, I told Carol, "Give me some time. I will do it, but I have to get my own life back in a good place. Right now I am too exhausted." Carol told me she didn't want me to give up a kidney. She knew I was already dealing with a lot.

In an effort to get her onto a transplant list, we would go to two of the largest hospitals in the state to see about putting Carol on that list. Upon talking with doctors at each hospital, one facility would not put her on the list because she didn't have a method of paying for the medication she would need for the rest of her life after the transplant. The other would not put her on the list because she continued to smoke.

A doctor she spoke with at one of the hospitals informed her that a virus had entered her body. This particular virus had attacked the kidneys and lungs. We knew exactly when she had become ill and when and where the virus had probably entered her body. Even with this knowledge, Carol said nothing to the dentist who had cleaned her teeth. She accepted her fate.

Even though the local hospital was only one block from Carol's home, she chose to do her dialysis at home. Independent as always, she was determined to do it herself. She had only been on dialysis a short time when she became very ill and had to be hospitalized. This time she was diagnosed with peritonitis.

Carol shared her apartment with two cats. Foolishly, she would let the cats on the bed as she was doing the dialysis. Infection, most probably from her cats, had entered her body. When she went home from the hospital, she knew she needed to be more careful with her dialysis.

Still living at home, Tina needed to have her own space. She liked to cook and was a good housekeeper. She usually kept things pretty clean and organized. When Tina stayed on her medication, she was quite capable of taking care of herself. The problem was that she would never accept she needed the medication and would often stop taking it.

Tina was no longer able to work forty hours a week. She qualified for housing assistance. Much to my surprise, Carol offered her upstairs apartment to Tina. I was thrilled. It hadn't even entered my mind. I wouldn't have been comfortable letting Tina move just anywhere, but I was at ease with the idea of Carol being downstairs. She could keep an eye on Tina.

I was surprised when Tina accepted Carol's offer, and she soon moved into the upstairs apartment. Although it was a relief for me at home, I still couldn't stop worrying about Tina, who was always on my mind.

In time, Carol had become too weak to continue working and would find it necessary to go onto disability. Carol always had so much pride. She enjoyed working and being around people. Disability could not have been an easy thing for her to accept. No longer able to work, Carol found it hard to survive on her small disability check. The meager amount of money she had in the bank was too much for her to qualify for food assistance.

Believing it would allow her to qualify for assistance if she spent some of her savings, she purchased a few things for her home. Next, she found the rent she received from Tina was considered income. She still didn't qualify for assistance. What was she supposed to do? She needed the rental income to make her house payment.

Unable to work, Carol was now home most of the time. Even though Tina was upstairs, Carol could hear her. Tina talked to the voices she constantly heard in her head. So often, when I would hear or see Tina doing this, it would break my heart. I so wished I could do more for her.

Unfortunately, in a very short time, I think Carol found living with Tina as stressful as I did. With all her disappointments, she really didn't need this. Carol couldn't get any assistance, make ends meet, or work, and because she hadn't quit smoking, she didn't qualify for a transplant. Nothing was going her way. How much disappointment could a person take?

Years earlier, Carol had moved to California without a job and about a hundred dollars. I would never have done something like that. She married while still in high school, something else I would never have done. Carol and I had always been so different. I would wonder, "How is she coping with all of this?" I was certain I couldn't deal with all of that stress and disappointment. Outwardly, she seemed to be coping. Carol didn't offer any clues as to how she felt.

I was working two jobs at the time, but neither were full time. I was doing office work at home for a local company, and I was also working for a moving company. Except for my experience with the custard stand and now the moving company, I had never done anything except office work. I decided I really didn't like to do office work. I quit the job I did at home.

I enjoyed the work I did for the moving company. We would go into people's homes and pack their belongings prior to their moving. I don't know if I liked the work or my coworkers. The women were good company, and we could talk while we worked, something one can't do very easily when doing office work. I found it relaxing.

After a full day of work, I would feel I needed to check on Carol and Tina every evening. I couldn't stop worrying about them until I had checked on their well-being. Carol did not like I felt the need to check on her continually. Still even knowing this, I couldn't stop myself.

Carol had been dealing with her kidney failure for less than two years when she once again became ill and had to be hospitalized. She was diagnosed with peritonitis for the second time. This time, it was much more serious than before. She was extremely ill and in unbearable pain.

This time, Carol would not leave the hospital. My brother and his girlfriend were with her when she passed away. When my brother called with the news, I could not believe she was gone. I think I was in a state of shock. For years, I had felt something before it would happen. I hadn't felt this coming. I knew the others were going to pass away, but I didn't expect this. I felt God had abandoned me. I was angry at Him. How could He do this?

CHAPTER 9

A few days after Carol passed away, we would have a small funeral for her. Tina wouldn't go to the service. She was in a world of her own. I had no idea what was going on in her mind. She didn't volunteer anything.

Carol had no will of any sort. The house would be left empty. We had no claim on it. Carol had no other relatives. My brother and nephews would remove her belongings. Tina would stay in the upstairs apartment a few weeks longer while we worked to make arrangements for her to move. I wanted Tina to live somewhere close to me so I could continue to check on her. We found a very nice apartment about one mile from home. As soon as we could, we moved Tina into her new residence.

I had quit talking to God on a regular basis after Carol passed. My faith had taken a blow. I felt lost. After feeling so close to God for so many years, I had closed my mind to Him as well. I didn't reach out to my friends. I didn't want to share anything with them, and I had nothing left to give them. With Carol gone, I didn't feel close to anyone.

When my family members had been sick, I would go for drives by myself. I wished I had a place I could go and just scream to release the emotions I was feeling. It had been so hard to watch them hurting and not being able to do anything to make their lives better.

It wasn't until after my younger sister was gone that I realized how much and how long I had been pushing myself. I had been running constantly for years. I no longer remembered what it was to sit down and not have something that needed my attention. I was unable to relax. I had witnessed my family endure so much pain for as long as I could remember. My mind was so full of pain. I knew I needed to get it out of my body. Carrying the extra baggage couldn't be healthy.

When I wasn't with Tina or my job, I would spend my spare time writing about my experiences with my family. This was my way of releasing my emotions. There had been so many disappointments over the years. They had endured so much, but to their credit, none of them had spent their time complaining about their illnesses.

As I wrote, I realized God had warned me of what was to come. He had cautioned me at least two times. But believing He couldn't possibly take anyone else from me, I had overlooked His messages. Unknowingly, because of the pain I felt from the loss of my other sister and my parents, with my mind closed, the messages had gone right past me.

Other than the time I spent working, writing, or staying with Tina, my only outlet was attending Melanie's college basketball games. She had received an athletic scholarship to a local college, and she was on the varsity basketball team. Melanie had also been asked to join the softball team, but she declined. She had played enough softball in high school. She no longer enjoyed it as she once had. She focused on her basketball instead.

While talking with a parent of one of Melanie's teammates, she asked if I would like to drive for their company. They offered a service much like a taxi. For example, they would offer rides to doctor appointments for the elderly. She set up an appointment for me with one of the other drivers. I rode with the lady as she picked up one elderly person after another, assisting them when necessary.

As I watched her help the elderly patients, my mind wandered to the many times I had done the same thing with my mother. The vivid memory was upsetting. She drove past my sister's now-empty house. It had been nearly two years since Carol passed away. I hadn't been near her home since we moved out Tina's belongings. This also upset me.

I began talking to the lady as she drove. I told her things I had not said to anyone in the years since Carol's passing. I was like a motor mouth. I couldn't stop talking about the things that hurt inside of me. Just like Tina, I had become isolated and hardly recognized myself. I knew I needed to get over mourning my family and join the world again.

I had spent hours writing. When I finished releasing all my hurt into those pages, I had nearly 150 pages of hurt, pain, and disappointment. But I was beginning to feel better about things. I was beginning to let go of the past.

After some time, believing I had an additional copy of my writing on my computer, I threw all those memories into the trash. I didn't ever want to relive that portion of my life. Years later, I discovered that I didn't have a copy of my writings. When I realized that segment of my life was gone forever, I thanked God I had thrown away those pages. Even now, years later, I can't and don't want to remember many of the things that happened in those years.

In the beginning, I had enjoyed my job with the moving company, but the working conditions kept changing. They were asking us to do more and more work with less help. When they scheduled a huge job involving a farmer who was moving south, they needed extra help. I had suggested that perhaps Tina could occasionally work with us. I knew Tina could never work more than one day at a time and explained that to them. Over the years, I had learned Tina's capacity for working. When she was tired, the voices in her head would take over, and she would be almost useless. She just could not function.

This particular day, Tina was with me. I had driven to the job thirty to forty miles from home. As I worked, one of the ladies came and told me Tina had left. Unable to cope with the environment, Tina had walked down the road. She could not have had any idea where she was going. Thank God I had driven to the job. I caught up with her and took her home.

Soon after that experience, I was expected to follow one of the men to a job. I had never driven the box truck. I always let one of the other ladies drive the truck to the job, but this morning I was alone. It was now eight in the morning, and I was driving through a construction zone with multiple lanes of traffic in an area of a city of which I was not familiar. And to top it all off, it was raining. I know my limitations, and I had no business driving that truck. I was not happy. They were putting my life and perhaps the life of someone else in jeopardy. No longer happy with my job, when the company decided to move their packing division to another city, I decided it was time to quit.

Over the years, Tina's condition continued to decline. Since I was no longer working, I would begin spending time with her every day. We would either go to breakfast or lunch.

Melanie's college basketball team had a tremendous year. They qualified for the national tournament, and were the last team to be invited to play in the tourney. We joined several parents of Melanie's teammates and attended.

While attending, a small group of us would take time each day and visit the Queen of Peace statue, a thirty-foot-high sculpture of the Virgin Mary. It is a beautiful piece of work. We were told, if we were to rub her feet, it would bring us luck. Each day, we would return to the statue and rub her feet.

Although we can't take all of the credit, our efforts must not have gone unnoticed. The girls won the tournament. They were the number-one team in their division that year.

Unable to keep a job for any length of time, Tina had gone on full disability. Working for even a short period of time would prove to be too much for her. Still firmly believing that nothing was wrong with her, Tina continued having trouble staying on her medication. When she wasn't taking her pills, she would be unable to function. She couldn't carry on a conversation without someone having to repeat himself or herself over and over again. She could never accept she needed her medication.

Years earlier, while still working, Tina had purchased a beautiful brown cocker spaniel who had been her companion for years. Once again, Tina was not taking her medication. When not on her pills, the voices would take over Tina's life. She would become obsessed with cleansing her body. Although she wouldn't take her medicine, she would consume multiple kinds of vitamins.

While in this state of mind, Tina began giving her dog vinegar water to drink. She was going to cleanse the dog as well. Of course, the dog wouldn't drink the foul-tasting water. Tina would put bowl cleaner into her toilet and not flush it. The dog would drink that water. I repeatedly asked her not to do this. In Tina's compromised state of mind, she couldn't understand what she was doing to her dog. Eventually Tina's beautiful dog hemorrhaged and died. Fortunately Tina would never understand what she had done to her dog.

On another occasion, she began spray-painting the apartment complex where she lived. She would spray-paint anything she felt needed freshening up. She went too far when she spray-painted the community mailboxes, which are federal property. You do not paint federal property. Her mental illness was the only thing that kept her from being charged.

Once Tina quit taking her medication, I could never get her to start taking it again. The voices would tell her not to take it, convincing her she didn't need it. At those times, the voices controlled Tina's life. The only way to get Tina back onto her medication would be when she was hospitalized. They would force her to take it.

Tina had been off her medication for quite some time. I was very concerned about her. She could no longer keep track of her bills. She was using a credit card to pay for pop and cigarettes. In addition to the cost of her purchases, there was a ten-dollar fee every time she used the card.

Years earlier, before being diagnosed as schizophrenic, Tina had gone bankrupt. She had only recently qualified for a credit card, and the cards she received were the worst ones out there. Her life was getting totally out of control. Concerned and unable to get Tina to begin taking her medicine, I visited the crisis center, asking for assistance. Unable to get anywhere constructive, I had left the crisis center and returned home.

I just entered the door at home when the phone rang. It was the crisis center. The girl said to me, "You are not going to believe this."

While I had been at the crisis center asking for help, Tina had gone to the police station and asked for help. She told them she was afraid of the voices. The police had taken her to the crisis center. Although not at all happy about the decision that was made for her, she was once again hospitalized and forced to take her medication.

CHAPTER 10

Tina had recently connected with a fellow she knew from high school, Kelly, and they had begun to keep in touch. Since I had been with Tina when she first ran into Kelly at a local gas station, I knew her new friend was a few years older than her. He seemed like a very nice person.

Melanie would graduate college soon. She would be the first member of our family to get a college degree. I was proud of her, as she had pretty much put herself through college with working and scholarships.

After Carol passed away, I had kept her ashes. Melanie suggested that both of us take a trip to California, back to where Carol was happiest, after her graduation. We were making arrangements to leave town. But before Melanie and I left for our trip, she and I paid a visit to Kelly. I wanted him to know what he was getting into with Tina. When I explained Tina's illness to Kelly, he understood. Kelly explained he had an uncle who was schizophrenic. No one with whom I communicated was familiar with schizophrenia. I felt it was destiny that Kelly came into our lives when he did.

Knowing how lonely Tina was, we asked Kelly to keep in touch with Tina while we were gone. He said he would. It was always really hard for me to leave Tina. I knew she was a grown adult, but much of her was still childlike. She was totally incapable of making sound judgments about things. She kept me on my toes, trying to keep her on an even keel. I knew I would worry about her and what she might do the entire time I was gone.

Before I left town, I wanted to let my neighbor know we would be out of town for a short while. Frieda had always followed Melanie's accomplishments. Frieda and I had one thing in common. In nearly the same time span as I had lost my sister, father, and mother, Frieda had lost her husband, mother, and son, her only child. Feeling her loss was even greater than mine kept me from feeling sorry for myself. Knowing she was usually alone, we had gotten into the habit of asking Frieda to join us for holidays and special occasions.

I usually spoke with Frieda on the phone. She would come to our house. I hadn't been inside her home for years. I went to her place to say good-bye. Once inside, I couldn't believe the disarray. It obviously hadn't been cleaned in many months. It suddenly became apparent she wasn't really doing well. The car was packed, and we were ready to leave. Feeling I should do something, I realized I could not do anything for her except run to the store for the food she requested.

Later that day, Melanie and I left. We drove until we needed gas. As I got out of the car to fill the tank, the music on the gas station speakers immediately got my attention. The song was "Babe." The words are, "I'm leaving. I must be on my way."

I got chills when I heard the song. I knew God was telling me something. As I often did, I went through a list of family members in my mind. When I hit the right person, I would usually feel it. I went through the entire family, and nothing hit. I didn't know for what I was being prepared.

I didn't have to wait long. When I called home the next day, I was greeted with the news that Frieda had passed away. Kris had come home for something. Someone knocked at the door, inquiring about Frieda. This person was concerned when he had gone to her door and didn't receive any response. Trying to help, Kris entered the house. She found Frieda. She had passed away. I was totally unprepared for this news. This was not the way to start a cross-country trip. Tina and Frieda would remain in my mind the entire time.

While we were gone, I would call Tina daily. After a few days, just as I had feared, Tina was losing touch with reality. What could I do? I was halfway across the country.

We drove each day until we were tired and stopped when it felt like it was the thing to do. When we reached California, we stayed with my aunt for a couple days. While there, we drove Carol's ashes to Mission Bay and released them. Carol had spent some of her happiest years at Mission Bay. Knowing how much Carol hated our hometown, I felt this was where she preferred to be.

We had driven across the center of the United States while going to California. We would return via the northern route. We saw so many national landmarks in such a short period of time. The only time we might have made a poor choice was when we decided to drive through the mountains in Wyoming and hadn't paid attention to the fact there were snowstorm warnings for the day.

I was still a naïve traveler. We were only partially up the mountain when the snow began. In a matter of minutes, a foot of snow was covering the road. Many places didn't have guardrails. We could no longer see the road. Then unbelievably, a snowplow made a U-turn right in front of us. While many people were stranded, we followed the snowplow out of the mountain.

As we entered Yellowstone National Park, no sooner did we drive up to Old Faithful before the geyser went off.

The entire trip was perfect. I repeatedly said, "Frieda and Carol are with us."

On the way through Iowa, we once again visited the Virgin Mary statue where we had been for Melanie's tournament. They had now also built a thirty-five-foot stainless steel monument of Jesus. It was beautiful the first time I saw it, and it was even lovelier now.

When I next spoke with Tina, I knew we needed to get home as soon as possible. Her birthday was in a few days. I knew she would be very disappointed if we were not home. That was the childlike part of Tina's personality. She would forever be sensitive about some things. So we would hurry the end of our trip in order to get home before her birthday. It was none too soon. Tina was getting worse every day.

Once Melanie and I had introduced ourselves to Kelly, he too had become a new member of our family. He was the best thing that ever happened to Tina or me. In the years to come, I appreciated all the things he did for my daughter. No matter what she needed him to do, he was always there for her and never let her down. Sometimes I would feel I just couldn't go on. I was so drained from dealing with Tina's ups and downs. It was then Kelly would remind me, "She can't help it." It helped so much just having someone understand.

Kris and Melanie had their own lives to live. Tina was not their priority. Dick stayed as uninvolved as possible. When Tina once again maxed out her credit cards and could no longer make the minimum payments, the calls from the collection agencies would begin, which would upset Tina, causing her to withdraw even more. Stress always made her illness worse. Although the calls upset her, it was not enough to ever teach her to stop using the cards. I would discover she had several cards she had maxed out. Trying to lessen the stress, I foolishly paid off the balances for her, with the warning, "Do not do this again." Unknown to me, Tina would almost immediately open a new account somewhere else.

Realizing Tina's mental condition was slowly worsening, I became her legal guardian. Not ever wanting to accept she had a problem, I was surprised Tina agreed to sign the papers, allowing me to do this. Dick and I would put our personal possessions into a trust so we could name Melanie to be in control of Tina's portion. It was our hope, when Dick and I were no longer here to look after Tina, Melanie would look after her.

When the facility Tina visited for her doctor appointments and medication closed, she would once again stop taking her pills. I had no one from whom to request assistance. Once again the voices would take over Tina's life. She began throwing her personal possessions into the dumpster at her apartment complex. One thing after another was disappearing.

When I became aware of the type of things she was throwing away, I began going to her complex at night and checking the dumpster. I simply could not afford to replace all the necessities she was tossing away. She had thrown away many of her clothes. One evening a friend accompanied me. Beneath an old mattress, we found Tina's birth certificate, utility bills, medical papers, and other various papers. She had previously thrown away her driver's license, which we had to replace. I assumed she believed, if she threw away her identification, she was getting rid of the person who was constantly talking to her in her head. She was always telling me that person was not her.

She wasn't done. She disconnected her stove and refrigerator. She removed everything from her cupboards and closets and put them into the center of her living room. She upset the bedroom furniture. When I saw what she had done, instead of contacting the crisis center, as I should have done, I cleaned her apartment. The next day, she had done the same thing. This time, Kelly helped her put things back.

When I again called the crisis center, explaining what she had been up to, they weren't able to help me. They needed to see what she had done. With the closure of the mental facility, there were others with conditions worse than Tina, so they took priority. They didn't feel she was a danger to herself or anyone else.

Shortly thereafter, Tina got into an argument with the landlord. I knew it was time to get something done before she was thrown out of her apartment. It took some time, but Tina once again would eventually be hospitalized. When she left the hospital this time, she told me, "That is the last time I am going there."

Upon her release, Tina would now receive her medical needs from a new facility and doctor. This time I had someone with whom I could speak. I liked her new doctor. For the first time, I felt she was in good hands.

From the very beginning, I had always gone with Tina to each of her appointments. She protested each time she had to go. This was the only way I could be sure she kept her appointments. She still believed nothing was wrong with her and she didn't need to go to the doctor.

Kris and her family had moved to Louisiana years earlier. When Dick, Melanie, her husband of a few years, Lance, and I wanted to visit Kris in Louisiana, I asked Tina to join us. I would never be able to go and leave Tina alone without anyone in the family to contact.

As with her father, change always upset Tina. She did not want to go. But after much pleading and coaxing, Tina finally agreed to it. Concerned about Tina's ability to control herself on the plane, I visited her doctor and asked about changing her medication. I explained I feared Tina would lose control on the plane and get all of us kicked off. The doctor changed her medication, and Tina showed a definite improvement. It was slight, but it was working better than the medication she had been taking. I was so grateful.

We made the trip without any problems. Tina handled the time away from home surprisingly well. We had a really nice time, and I was so glad she went with us.

But just when I would think we had turned a corner, Tina would again refuse to take her medication. I visited her doctor, explaining to him, in her mind, she no longer needed medication and would no longer willingly take it. The doctor allowed me to fill her prescriptions, and Tina never knew I was spiking her drinks with her medication.

I would crush her pills, dissolve them, and add them to her drink when she was not looking. It was something of which I was not proud, but it was keeping her out of the hospital. This worked for nearly one year, but all good things must come to an end.

Someone from the facility who oversaw the prescriptions that patients were receiving called Tina. When Tina said she hadn't filled her prescriptions, the woman told her someone was. Tina called and asked, "Are you filling my prescriptions?" I told her I was. I explained to her, "I don't want to be around you if you aren't on your medication."

For the first time, she willingly started taking the medicine. She later stated the only reason she did was because I said I didn't want to be around her if she didn't. After all these years, why didn't I think of that sooner?

CHAPTER 11

Not long after I had paid off Tina's credit cards, I discovered she had once again maxed out new ones. I was terribly disappointed. This time I was not about to be foolish enough to pay them a second time. Instead I wrote to each creditor, explaining, if they had taken the time to check her credit rating, they would have known she shouldn't have qualified for a credit card. I stated she was mentally ill and lived on disability. The creditors graciously wrote off the balance to her accounts.

I felt perhaps stopping the phone calls regarding her unpaid balances would take the pressure off Tina. I was constantly trying to make my daughter's life as stress-free as possible. I knew Tina felt badly about what she had done, but she just couldn't stop herself. They sent the applications via mail. They made it easy for her to get a card, and she couldn't turn down the offer.

Having removed the tension from her life, due to phone calls about unpaid credit card balances, things seemed to go a little more smoothly. I believed she was really trying to improve her way of life. She would often feel down because her sisters had so much and she had nothing. She wanted to be married and have a family, as they did.

At these times, I would tell her, "Don't look at all the people who have more than you. Look at all the people who don't have as much as you do. Between your disability check and the assistance you receive, you don't have to worry about having a roof over your head. That is a lot more than many people have."

I would often wonder why some people have life so good and others struggle. In my heart, I believe we all have just what we are supposed to have. I believe my own life choices have been something I needed to do to free my soul from guilt I felt from my last life.

It is my belief I was my grandmother in my last life. When forced to choose between my children and my father, I left my children and went out West to look after my father. My daughter, my mother in this lifetime, had to pretty much raise her three brothers. In my previous life, I died in my early forties of stomach cancer. I believe my guilt and inability to make peace with myself brought on the cancer. And I believe this because I am basically the same person in this life. Except in this lifetime, I think I have my priorities, that is, my immediate family, straight.

I would awaken, and little by little, these things would be revealed to me. I know how hard this is for many to believe. It happened to me, and I cannot believe it occurred. Many won't believe my version of life, but I am 100 percent comfortable with my beliefs. And only God knows the truth.

It was Wednesday, my seventy-second birthday. I picked up Tina, as usual, that morning. For years, she and I had visited the Goodwill stores in our area. Although I couldn't afford to buy Tina things at full price, the Goodwill stores were affordable. It would lift Tina's spirits to have something new to look at or wear.

We were going to K-Mart this morning instead of our usual visit to the Goodwill stores. Tina wasn't feeling well. She had been coughing a lot. She had been for months. Again that morning, I warned her she was going to be unable to breathe freely or go out in the cold, like my father and brother. She would just get frustrated at hearing the same old words.

At K-Mart, as I went and looked for what I needed, Tina stayed at the jewelry counter. When I returned, she had tried on a ring of emerald and diamonds, her birthstone. She begged me, "Could I please have this for my birthday this year?"

It was March. Her birthday wasn't until May. It was a pretty ring. I told her I would think about it and walked off. As I walked, I was asking my conscience, "Should I buy the ring?"

Years ago, I had gotten into the habit of asking my guiding voice about unnecessary purchases. It helped me to stay on my budget without worrying about having enough money next month to make ends meet. Surprisingly it felt like the right thing to do, and I bought Tina her birthstone ring.

We were going to Melanie and Lance's for dinner that evening. It was unusual for Mel to ask us to dinner, but since it was my birthday, I didn't think too much of it.

After finishing dinner, we were relaxing at the table. Melanie handed me a picture. As I looked at it, I realized it was a sonogram. I smiled. It was her way of telling me she was expecting. She and Lance were going to become parents. I was very pleased and pleasantly surprised. We hadn't had a baby in the family for so long. My other two grandchildren were now in their twenties and lived in Louisiana. Now I understood why I kept my high chair. I was going to need it.

Tina didn't say much. Once again, one of her sisters was going to enjoy something she never would. Although glad for Melanie's good fortune, I could feel the sadness it caused Tina. She wanted a husband, a nice home, and a family, but at forty-seven, it didn't seem likely to be in her future.

A day or so after Melanie's news, I could feel something was wrong. Often when someone close to me was troubled, I would be able to feel the unrest in my body. In my mind, I would start with one person and go through the family until I would know who was troubled about something. This morning I was experiencing that sort of feeling.

Tina and I were in the car, returning from our usual morning together. I was just about to drop off Tina at her apartment. I said to Tina, "Something is wrong. I can feel it."

Again I silently in my mind went through everyone's name, and when I said "Tina," I knew who was troubled. I looked at her as I told her I knew it was her. She didn't say anything. She didn't deny it; nor did she offer an explanation. I dropped her off and went home. I would find out soon enough what was troubling her. She wasn't ready to talk about it.

On Sunday, when we usually made the Goodwill run, Tina said she wanted to stay home. She wasn't feeling well. I was worried about her, but I was always concerned for her. When she got into these moods, she would quit taking her medication, and then life would go to hell again.

Later in the day, wanting to keep her in a pleasant frame of mind, I picked up a couple of lighthearted movies for her to watch and took them to her apartment. I didn't stay long. When Tina was in this frame of mind, I felt she preferred to be alone.

The next morning was Monday, March 24. I stopped over to pick up the movies that were due back. Still not feeling well, Tina didn't want to go anywhere. Tina said, "I ordered something for your birthday. It should have been here by now. I want to wait for the mail." Whatever it was, she felt it was something I needed, and she wanted me to have it. I had told her numerous times, "I don't need a thing."

For the past week, Tina's legs and ankles had been swollen. I had checked her blood pressure a few days earlier, and it was high. But considering the amount of Diet Coke she drank and the mini cigars she smoked, I wasn't sure what her blood pressure should be.

In the past few months, I had suggested numerous times that she go to the doctor. She refused. Kelly also had offered to pay for a doctor appointment for her. She refused. Like me, Tina didn't like doctors. She promised she would go when she received her disability check at the beginning of April. That was only a week or so away, so this time I didn't say anything.

She mumbled something about not needing to take the medication she was on. I was so familiar with this mood. It usually preceded her decision to quit taking the meds. I didn't stay long and left.

That afternoon, I called Kris in Louisiana. As I spoke with her, I said, "I feel as though we are going to lose Tina." Kris was quick to tell me, "I think you are wrong. I don't feel any such thing. Once I hung up the phone, I didn't think any more about the feeling I had regarding Tina. It had completely left my mind.

I didn't call Tina on Tuesday. If she wanted to go anywhere, she would have called me. When she was in her moods of not needing her meds, it was best for me to let her alone. I only added to her frustration of having to take medication.

On Tuesday night, I picked up my phone, and for absolutely no reason, Tina's phone number appeared on my phone. I thought that was strange. I had never noticed my phone doing this before. I thought about calling Tina but chose not to. I was going to go over first thing the next morning.

The next morning, I called Tina's apartment. There was no answer. In the past, sometimes when she was off her medication, she wouldn't answer the phone. Believing perhaps that was the case, before I left for Tina's apartment, I took the time to mix her medication in the tiny container I used to slip her the medicine she needed.

When I reached her apartment, I knocked on the door. There was no answer. I tried the door. It was unlocked. For nearly fifteen years, I had gone to Tina's apartment. It had never been unlocked. I let myself into her apartment. I noticed she wasn't in the kitchen or living area. I went to her bedroom. Tina was lying on her bed. As I walked to her bed, I noticed her coloring. She was purple. My heart sank. I touched her. She was so cold and hard. I knew immediately she was gone.

I had never made an emergency phone call in my life. It took a little time for me to figure out what I needed to do. Do I dial the area code before 9-1-1? One's mind goes blank when one walks into something like this. I was shaking as I dialed 9-1-1.

As I spoke to the operator, I couldn't remember the name of Tina's apartment complex or her apartment number. I told her the streets that intersected her apartment and said I would watch for them. Even though two days before I felt we might lose Tina, it was the very last thing on my mind that morning as I entered her apartment. I never dreamed we would lose her so soon.

I looked at Tina. It was as though she had just drifted off. Her hands were under her head. Her fingers were straight and touching, as they would have been had she been praying. She looked so peaceful. She was still wearing the same clothes she wore when I saw her on Monday morning.

Shaking, I called my husband and daughter and told them they needed to come to Tina's as soon as possible. The items I took to Tina's on Monday were still right where I set them. I believe she went into her bedroom when I left and passed away soon after, which was why the door was still unlocked.

As they removed Tina from her apartment, I could not look. I kept my back to what they were doing. I began to sob as I had never cried before in my life. There was no doubt I knew this was what God had prepared me for so many years earlier.

CHAPTER 12

E ven though for many years I didn't completely understand what God was trying to tell me, He had taken me through this day so many times. For many years, I had known there was going to be an earth-shattering event in my lifetime. I knew this was it.

As much as I feared this day, the totally surprising thing was the way I felt in the days following finding Tina. Instead of the horrific pain I had always feared would take over my body, the only thing I could feel was Tina's complete peace and happiness. It was actually a beautiful time. I knew Tina was in a good place. I could feel her happiness and hear her laughing. As much as everyone around me didn't believe me, I also knew Tina was not going to be gone long. I knew this was a gift from God and I was experiencing something very special. This time I was not going to close my mind.

I knew this was why I always felt pregnant after experiencing the death. I knew God was sending her back to me via her sister. Tina would never be back, but I had no doubt God was sending Tina's soul back to me. Melanie was going to look after Tina, but in a completely different set of circumstances than what I had foreseen. Once again, God knew best.

I could not believe the feelings I was experiencing. I never felt closer to God. He cared enough about me to warn me so long ago about this period in my life. I felt like the luckiest person in the world. I wouldn't spend my days mourning the loss of my daughter. How could I? She hated most everything about her life. I remembered the time she told me, "You don't understand. The voices never go away." And I would wonder, "Why is the occasional voice I hear always a positive one while Tina hears voices constantly and those she perceives are destructive?" I would have to be selfish to want her back in such an unhappy life. Those voices were now silent for her. She was now happy and free.

For three days, my mind never turned off. I felt I was doing well, but I must not have been. Even though my mind was not turning off, my body must have been sleeping. The first night after finding Tina, I was awakened about three o'clock in the morning.

The voice said to me, "You can't go yet. You aren't done."

The second night, again I was awakened about three o'clock in the morning. It was the same message, "You can't go yet. You aren't done."

Did I quit breathing? I didn't feel as though I had been sleeping, but I must have been. Why was I being awakened with this message?

Because it was necessary to have an autopsy, the services for Tina would be delayed. It gave me time to deal with the shock of the moment. Kris, her husband, and their children also needed time to come home from Louisiana.

Melanie and I needed to clear Tina's apartment. It was the end of the month. Her next month's rent would be due soon. As we were busy packing her belongings, we paused for a break. I was telling Melanie how I had previously told Tina, if she ever smelled as bad as my brother (because of the smoking), I was going to tell her about it. The words were no more out of my mouth than the air freshener in Tina's apartment went *pshhhh!*

Melanie and I looked at one another and laughed. I felt Tina's spirit was definitely in the room with us.

As I was gathering Tina's paperwork, one paper fell out. As I picked it up, I realized it was a balance due on another credit card. The previous year, I had taken care of her charge cards. I had written to each creditor involved, explained her situation, and believed the accounts had all been closed. I preached to her over and over again, "Don't use credit cards. I will give you the money if you need it." But as she always had in the past, she had once again opened a new credit account.

As we finished packing her belongings and headed home, we reached the intersection near my house. At that moment, I could feel Tina with me so strongly. She was so happy, and I could hear her laughing. It was such a beautiful and comforting feeling, knowing she was so at peace.

A day later, Larry's sister sent her sons and their trucks to empty Tina's apartment. It took five guys about one hour to move her belongings from her apartment to our garage. She also sent enough food for three complete meals for our entire family.

Until I could have her mail transferred to my home address, each day I would check for Tina's mail. Kris was now home, and this time, she went with me. As I sorted Tina's mail, I would realize why God had sent Kris with me this time. I saw another credit card bill, and this one had a much larger balance due than the first one I had found. My heart dropped. I knew this was the feeling I had experienced when, less than a week earlier, I said to Tina that something was wrong. She had once again overextended herself with credit cards. Since I knew how sensitive Tina was, she wouldn't have wanted me to know. She knew I would be disappointed in her. Yes, I would have been, but I also would have forgiven her.

Another day later, I saw two credit card cases in Tina's mail, one for each of us. I knew this was the gift for me. I hated credit cards. I thought, *why would she buy something like that for my birthday?* I believe it was God's way of explaining to me what was once again troubling Tina.

Since I always felt I wanted to be cremated, we decided we were also going to have Tina cremated. I had always hated the idea of putting a body into the ground. I wanted her with me, not in the ground somewhere.

Kris and I were relaxing in the living room when I decided to clear the coffee table. The last few days had been hectic, to say the least. As I cleared the papers, I picked up the receipt for Tina's birthday ring. Until I saw the date on the receipt, it hadn't occurred to me that I bought her birthstone ring on my own birthday, the day Melanie announced she was pregnant. I believed this was God's way of again reassuring me that He was sending her back to me.

On the morning of Tina's service, I awoke with a message from God. During my sleep, He explained the signs of the cross. Catholics repeat the signs of the cross, "In the name of the Father, the Son, and the Holy Spirit." God said to me, "What we think (touch the forehead), what we eat (touch the stomach), and what we do (touch one shoulder and then the other), all must be in harmony. Before we can hear God and truly follow Him and not ourselves, all of these things must be in order. To me, this made so much sense. I understood exactly what He meant. It was exactly what He had been teaching me the last forty years.

The morning of Tina's services, I had gotten out of bed and dressed first. I was dressed in purple. When I went into the living room, I was surprised to see Kris had slept on the sofa. I had awakened her. As Kris dressed, I teased her when I saw she also had chosen a purple outfit.

The night before, after I had gone to bed, my grandson Shane arrived from Louisiana. I had not yet seen him. Realizing

Shane had left Louisiana without proper dress clothing, Kris had purchased a new shirt and slacks for him. As Shane pulled his clothes out of his travel bag, I noticed he had chosen a purple plaid shirt. When I saw he too had chosen purple clothes, I told him, "Wear the clothes you brought. I want you to be you."

Then I noticed my granddaughter had chosen a tie with purple in it for her father. Dick's tie also had purple in it.

Over the years, so often Tina and I would be dressed alike. I would pick her up in the morning, only to find we looked as though we had planned our wardrobes. I would tease her, telling her not to walk with me. We looked strange, so often dressed alike. The morning of Tina's funeral, I believed my daughter had helped us pick our clothing choices. She probably knew I would pick up on it. Once again, I knew she was with all of us.

Since I didn't feel I could face a bunch of people, we chose to have a small service for family and a few of our closest friends. Dick's family alone would nearly fill the room for her service. I have few remaining relatives.

As we arrived at the funeral home, I shared our clothing issue with the director. As we talked, the deacon who was going to speak at the service walked into the room. The funeral director stated, "I don't believe it." When I looked at the deacon, he also had on a purple shirt and a purple tie.

As I stood in the line, greeting our family and friends, the silent voice that had become so much a part of me was now talking to me. It said, "You are going to write about this."

The day before Tina's service, Kelly had told us what he had prepared to say. The day of, when he started to speak, he had forgotten his notes. It didn't matter. Kelly could not have delivered a more perfect memorial of his experiences with Tina. I wish I had a copy of the things he said. He made her service perfect. Kelly stated he felt God had put him in Tina's life. I am 100 percent certain God put Kelly in our lives.

Tina and Kelly's relationship was more a sister-brother relationship, not a romantic one. He and Tina would often come to the house, and we played cards or went out to eat. Kelly couldn't have been a better friend than he was to Tina. So often through the years, I thanked God for Kelly's assistance in dealing with Tina. He had become Dick's favorite hunting buddy. My daughters called him their brother. I felt he was the son I never had.

Dick and I had each requested a song to be played during the service. They played the song Dick requested several times but never played "Amazing Grace," as I had requested. I wondered why but said nothing. We had arrived at the funeral home earlier than expected. I doubt they had time to get organized like they would have preferred.

When I spoke of this later with Kris, I would receive my answer. She said, "I couldn't have handled it if they played 'Amazing Grace.' They played that at Larry's funeral. It would have been too much."

After the service, everyone met at Melanie's house. I didn't worry about what we were going to do or feed our family and friends after the service. Melanie's neighbors all pitched in and helped organize things. We had plenty of food, and everything went unbelievably smooth.

We returned home after Tina's services and lunch. My two grandkids were on the sofa, teasing one another. As I watched them enjoying the moment, I would have another flash. I hadn't had one in a very long time.

Instead of my grandkids sitting there having a good time, it was my father and sister, Pat. I was very hesitant to share this with others, as I too have a hard time believing it happened, but it did. That is the beauty of God. We never know what to expect or when.

A day or so after Tina's services, I was looking at the

arrangement that the family of Melanie's husband had sent. As soon as I saw it, I noticed a Willow Tree figurine in the center. They were Tina's favorites. As I removed the figurine from the plant, I noticed it was a music box. I wound the box. The tune was "Amazing Grace." That was a beautiful moment. It was as though Tina herself had picked it out at the florists, and I believe she probably did.

A week or so later, I went to lunch with my school friends. They had purchased a memorial snow globe. It too was a music box and had a space at the top for a picture of a loved one. The card I had sent to thank friends for their thoughtfulness in the previous days contained a picture of Tina. The picture fit into the music box, like it was made for it. The music box also played "Amazing Grace."

It took forty-plus years, but God explained both of my visions to me. It taught me just how loving and caring He is. I no longer fear the unknown. I know God will prepare me for anything that could upset my world. He truly took care of everything. I realize how in control of everything God is. Again it was unbelievable.

About a week after Tina's service, I went for a drive. Suddenly, the voice said to me, "I am the Father, you are the Son, and the Holy Spirit is the part of you that is reborn until you reach perfection."

I couldn't believe what just happened. That made so much sense. I got so excited and asked "Why me? Why do I receive messages no one else does?"

CHAPTER 13

When we received the papers from the coroner, it was determined Tina had died of walking pneumonia. That was why she had been coughing for months. Many years earlier, the psychic had told me I was going to lose someone close to me, and the person had dark brown hair. At that time, Tina was only a child and had light brown hair. Over the years, her hair had turned a very dark brown.

Today I believe God knows when He is taking us back when we are born. I know we don't have to speak out loud for Him to know what we are thinking. I believe He knows everything we are going to do long before we do it.

I have come a long way from the nonbeliever I once was. But even now, I don't like to listen to someone preach. I know I wouldn't be fooling God. He knows exactly how I feel about things, and He has been so good to me.

Before Tina's passing, I had previously mentioned to friends that I would spend the spring cleaning out my flower beds at home. It had been so long since I stayed home and took care of them. They were completely out of control. I had expressed concern about what Tina would do because I wouldn't be going over every morning to pick her up. God is always a step ahead of me. He already knew Tina wouldn't be here and already had something to fill my time.

It would take months for me to clear the ground cover that had overtaken my numerous flower beds. As I worked, I felt Tina with me every day during those months. It was so comforting to be able to feel her presence.

Whenever I began to miss her, I was instantaneously reminded that she would be back. God never let me dwell on the fact she was no longer with me. It was so strange. This was not at all how one should feel when he or she loses someone he or she loves. Tina was someone I had been with nearly every day for the past fifteen years. I knew I was feeling something very out of the ordinary. Again I felt so blessed.

Dick was trimming his apple trees. He wanted me to pick up the branches and put them on a burn pile. I had already made plans to visit a friend. She had lost her husband the previous year. I was not about to change my plans. I felt I was doing what I was supposed to be doing that morning. As I left, I knew Dick was upset with my decision not to stay home and help him.

When I returned, unknown to Dick at the time, he had lost his glasses and his hearing aid. As he was throwing the branches into the fire, they had fallen off his head and into the fire. When we found the glasses, they were burnt beyond recognition. The hearing aid would never be found. Although Dick is the one who goes to church every Sunday, I knew, like many, he doesn't "see," and he doesn't "hear."

The summer passed rather quickly. It was time to plan a baby shower for Melanie and the new baby. Kris was coming home from Louisiana for the shower. When Dick and I picked her up at the airport, she wasn't feeling very well. She hadn't eaten all day. Perhaps that was why she didn't feel well. We took her to her favorite restaurant, but she couldn't eat. Her husband had been out of the country on business, and she was upset about flying home alone. I thought maybe that was upsetting her.

Dan was back the next day. She was getting worse. We told her she needed to see a doctor. She wouldn't budge. She wasn't going, and that was all there was to it.

Days passed, and she hadn't been able to eat anything or keep fluids down. Something was very wrong.

The day of the baby shower, Kris didn't go to Melanie's. She had come home for the baby shower and was too sick to attend. I went alone.

Surprisingly during the baby shower, Kris found enough strength to come to Melanie's house for the shower. She didn't look well. She didn't seem to be able to grasp what was going on around her. She seemed to be in a daze. She was determined she was not going to the doctor.

When I awoke the next morning, I had the feeling Kris's organs could begin to shut down if she didn't get help. When Dan got up, I mentioned this to him.

His reply really surprised me, "They already are shutting down. She wet the bed last night."

Dan, Dick, and I all told Kris, "You are going to the emergency room."

She was still determined she wasn't going.

Finally her father very firmly said, "Kris, you *are* going."

She relented and went to the emergency room. She would spend the next ten days in the intensive care unit. She had infections in her liver, blood, and kidneys. She also had two types of pneumonia. She was very sick.

When we visited, we were required to wear a clean smock, gloves, and mask each and every time we entered and exited her room. When I saw her, barely any space was left in her room. It was full of machinery.

While everyone was terribly anxious over her condition, I could feel God within me so strongly. He told me Kris was going to be fine. I felt at peace inside. There was no anxiety. When

Kris' daughter called to check on her mother, even though I knew Kris was seriously ill, I assured her, "Your mom is going to be fine. I wouldn't tell you that if I weren't sure."

During the days Kris was in intensive care, I could not convince Melanie she would not lose another sister. We had lost Tina the end of March. It was now September. Melanie was extremely stressed. The baby wasn't due for another month.

After nearly two weeks, Kris finally left the hospital. And as Kris left, Melanie went in. The stress was too much for Melanie. She went into early labor. The baby was born three weeks early.

When Kailee Marie was born, she made eye contact almost immediately. She smiled all the time. It seemed she understood everything we said to her. She was the happiest, most alert newborn I had ever seen.

While visiting at Melanie's a few weeks later, Kelly touched the baby on the end of her nose with his finger, something I had seen him do to Tina numerous times. At that time, Tina would close her eyes and turn her head.

When the baby closed her eyes and turned her head, just as I had seen Tina do, I knew for certain Tina was back. For me, it was a beautiful and special moment. Every time I see the baby do something Tina used to do, I realize how blessed I am. It is as though God is reassuring me, "Yes, it is her."

I feel so fortunate. I only wish everyone could experience the things I have since I found God. Then everyone would know how beautiful life on earth can actually be. It will be that way for all of us once we close our minds to the devil and follow the guidance available to us from God, if only we open our minds and let His messages in.

Death erases all of the hurtful memories or experiences we have endured. We will come back with a fresh, new outlook about life. Some of our old habits will remain, but a few of the negative traits we learned to overcome will not repeat in our next lifetime.

I no longer view death as the end, but a new beginning. Very few of us are perfect, so most of us will be reborn. Some will come sooner than others, but nevertheless, the majority of us will be back.

Our destiny lies in our hands. It is solely up to us what we choose to learn and overlook. Every cloud has a silver lining. Although my marriage didn't live up to my expectations, I don't regret things. God knew what He was doing. While many will spend their entire life leaning on their husband or wife, I know I can handle life on my own. Perhaps I would never have found God and turned to Him in times of trouble if I had been leaning on someone else.

My husband very much helped to make me the person I am. I am strong and independent. Emotionally I know I don't need another to get me through life. Whatever the future holds for me, I know God will be with me every step of the way.

I don't regret the things I haven't seen or done in this lifetime. I will have the time and opportunity to do them in the next. Nothing I could have chosen to do would have given me the peace of mind I now have. I would do everything the same way again.

Because God helped me tremendously through the thing I probably feared the most—the loss of a child—I feel I am free.

Printed in the United States
By Bookmasters